The Heart *of* Things

Richard Holloway was Bishop of Edinburgh and Primus of the Scottish Episcopal Church. A former Gresham Professor of Divinity and Chairman of the Joint Board of the Scottish Arts Council and Scottish Screen, he is a fellow of the Royal Society of Edinburgh. *Leaving Alexandria* won the PEN/Ackerley Prize and was shortlisted for the Orwell Prize. It was a *Sunday Times* bestseller, together with *Waiting for the Last Bus.*

Also by Richard Holloway

Let God Arise (1972)

New Vision of Glory (1974)

A New Heaven (1979)

Beyond Belief (1981)

Signs of Glory (1982)

The Killing (1984)

The Anglican Tradition (ed.) (1984)

Paradoxes of Christian Faith and Life (1984)

The Sidelong Glance (1985)

The Way of the Cross (1986)

Seven to Flee, Seven to Follow (1986)

Crossfire: Faith and Doubt in an Age of Certainty (1988)

The Divine Risk (ed.) (1990)

Another Country, Another King (1991)

Who Needs Feminism? (ed.) (1991)

Anger, Sex, Doubt and Death (1992)

The Stranger in the Wings (1994)

Churches and How to Survive Them (1994)

Behold Your King (1995)

Limping Towards the Sunrise (1996)

Dancing on the Edge (1997)

Godless Morality: Keeping Religion Out of Ethics (1999)

Doubts and Loves: What Is Left of Christianity (2001)

On Forgiveness: How Can We Forgive the Unforgiveable? (2002)

Looking in the Distance: The Human Search for Meaning (2004)

How to Read the Bible (2006)

Between the Monster and the Saint:
Reflections on the Human Condition (2008)

Leaving Alexandria: A Memoir of Faith and Doubt (2012)

A Little History of Religion (2016)

Waiting for the Last Bus (2018)

Stories We Tell Ourselves (2020)

The Heart of Things

On Memory & Lament

Richard Holloway

CANONGATE

This paperback edition published in 2022 by Canongate Books

First published in Great Britain, the USA and Canada in 2021
by Canongate Books Ltd, 14 High Street, Edinburgh EH1 1TE

Distributed in the USA by Publishers Group West
and in Canada by Publishers Group Canada

canongate.co.uk

1

British Library Cataloguing-in-Publication Data
A catalogue record for this book is available on
request from the British Library

ISBN 978 1 83885 497 3

Typeset in Garamond MT by
Palimpsest Book Production Ltd, Falkirk, Stirlingshire

Printed and bound in Great Britain by Clays Ltd, Elcograf S.p.A.

MIX
Paper from
responsible sources
FSC
www.fsc.org   FSC® C018072

For Alastair Hulbert

I saw rain falling and a rainbow drawn on Lammermuir.
Hearkening, I heard again in my precipitous city,
Beaten bells winnow the keen, sea wind,
And here afar, intent on my own race and place, I wrote.

Robert Louis Stevenson

CONTENTS

Preface   xi

   I   Passing   1
  II   Mourning   22
 III   Warring   40
 IV   Ruining   65
  V   Regretting   90
 VI   Forgiving   116

Endnotes   149
Acknowledgements   157
Permission Credits   159
Image Credits   162

PREFACE

Years ago, a friend said of my books that they were a multitude of quotations loosely connected along a string of commentary from me. I was only slightly annoyed and replied that, on the whole, that's what non-fiction writing was. It was a conversation or an argument with other writers. It was a link in a long chain of reflection that might go back centuries, since most of the important arguments that humans have with each other are rarely concluded, though they may twist in a different direction. Think of the hundreds of books written about the Bible each year, I went on, commentary on texts that were themselves thousands of years old. So-called *creative* writing was different, which is why it was called *fiction*, meaning made-up or imagined.

Now I am not so sure of the distinction I was making between non-fiction and fiction. And not just because a self-conscious new literary genre has emerged in recent years, what we might call creative non-fiction, sometimes called, in a dull phrase, *faction* – a combination of fact and fiction, or fact fictionalised. Anyway, it is not so new. St Augustine's autobiography, *Confessions,* reads like a novel because it *was* a novel, the story of a life creatively written, fictionalised, dramatised. Memoir is always like this. It is not a clinical accumulation of facts; it is the search for an identity, an attempt to understand a life. To that extent, it is a bit like Freudian analysis, the uncovering of events, buried or forgotten, that determined the shape of the life that followed, the life it helped to make up.

I have already written that kind of memoir, *Leaving Alexandria*.[1] This book is different. It is what is called an *anthology*, as the word suggests, a gathering of flowers plucked from other people's gardens. But it is like a memoir, in that it is also a search for the influences of other writers on the life of the author. Especially poets. *Poetry* is another of those words whose meaning we have to be creative about. It comes from the Greek *to make*. Make what? Well, among other meanings, to make present again what is past, bring it back to mind, *remember* it. While compiling this anthology of other writers' memories, I found myself composing remembrances of my own, some of which I have inserted into this text, like pictures in a photograph album. In this the art of poetry is like the art of photography, a point made by Philip Larkin, one of the poets anthologised in this book, himself a master of both.

Still with Larkin, when I pick up his wonderful curation of poetry, *The Oxford Book of Twentieth Century English Verse*, it always opens at the same page, because it holds a long stem of dried lavender that I placed there years ago to mark my first reading of what is now an important poem to me, 'The Burning of the Leaves', by Laurence Binyon. That's what an anthology is. That's what an anthology does. It is a collection of poetic flowers that saved or enlarged the life of the reader. This is my collection. But I'll leave the last word to Michel de Montaigne, history's greatest anthologist.

It could be said of me that in this book I have only made up a bunch of other men's flowers, providing of my own only the string that ties them together.[2]

Like Montaigne, I'm fine with that.

PASSING

A surprising number of people don't like the word 'passing' used for 'dying'. They see it as an act of avoidance or cowardice, a refusal to face facts. She hasn't *passed*, they say, she's *dead,* she's *gone*, she has been utterly extinguished, snuffed out like a candle. Apart from being irritated by the pedanticism of the complaint – after all, everyone knows what the word means in this context – I actually like using passing for, or as well as, dying, for a couple of reasons. The first is that I sympathise with the urge to soften the subject, or to gloss over it, disguise it. Sometimes we are just not able to take in the sudden and harsh reality of death. That is why we have not only invented euphemisms to soften its impact, we have gone even further and denied its finality by persuading ourselves that death was not an end, it was a door to another room.

Our beloved dead have not left us for ever. They have passed on or passed through this life to another life beyond, where we will meet them again when our own time comes. It takes a mean spirit and a narrow heart to deny the bereaved the comfort of this kind of hope. It is so persistent in human experience that only the invincibly ungenerous would deny the consolation it promises. And it is testimony to the existential impossibility many find in accepting that someone they had loved utterly and dependently could just disappear like that. King Lear caught the tone at the death of his daughter Cordelia in the cry: Thou'lt come no more, Never, never, never, never, never! The word *passing*, far from being weak and evasive, seems to me to catch the complex feel of dying.

But my other reason for liking the word is that, as well as catching the feel of human death, it captures the feel of human life. *Passing* is what life also feels like, because it is what time does, and time is the medium in which we have our being – till it runs out on us, and we stop.

The thought of time widening behind us like the wake of a ship, and diminishing in front of us as we draw close to port, can prompt the kind of reflective sorrow we call melancholy, a mood that has to be distinguished from its grim cousin, depression. Melancholy is what I am writing about here; melancholy, the mood that invades us when we realise how time is drifting away from us into the past, always into the past.

On Sundays,
    when the rain held off,
    after lunch or later,
    I would go with my twelve year old
    daughter into town,
    and put down the time
    at junk sales, antique fairs.

There I would
lean over tables,
absorbed by
lace, wooden frames,
glass. My daughter stood
at the other end of the room,
her flame-coloured hair
obvious whenever –
which was not often –

I turned around.
I turned around.
She was gone.
Grown. No longer ready
to come with me, whenever
a dry Sunday
held out its promises
of small histories. Endings.

When I was young
I studied styles: their use
and origin. Which age
was known for which
ornament: and was always drawn
to a lyric speech, a civil tone.
But never thought
I would have the need,
as I do now, for a darker one.

Spirit of irony,
my caustic author
of the past, of memory, –

and of its pain, which returns
hurts, stings – reproach me now,
remind me
that I was in those rooms,
with my child,
with my back turned to her,
searching – oh irony! –
for beautiful things.[1]

This poem has the classic marks of the state we call melancholy, an almost pleasurable sadness at the memory of the loss of a person or a place; a grateful mourning, an affectionate regret, a tender sorrow. It is a mood I am prone to, and it is one I find in many poets and other writers, so I am in interesting company. When I was reading Jan Morris's *Trieste and the Meaning of Nowhere*, I was pleased to discover that the philosopher Aristotle thought all interesting people had a touch of melancholy in their make up. However, 'melancholy' is a word with a past, and we can't just take it as we understand it today without thinking about its history. Words are dynamic realities that keep shifting their meaning, and *melancholy* is a good example of this verbal dynamism.

It began life as a term associated with the Greek physician and father of medicine, Hippocrates (460–370 BCE) – based on the ancient theory of the four elements or 'humours' – that described one of the quartet of human temperaments that were believed to control not only our biology but our personalities as well. They were: phlegm, blood, choler and black bile. Following this classification, we get the *phlegmatic* or apathetic person, the *sanguine* or enthusiastic person, the *choleric* or bad-tempered person, and the *melancholic* or depressed person, each formed by the humour that dominated their biological make up. In the case of the melancholic, the dominant element was believed to be black bile, in Greek, *melan-cholia*. Reading that, I don't like the sound of it. And as someone who occasionally suffers from acid reflux, I don't like the feel of it either. My dictionary describes bile as 'a bitter greenish-brown alkaline fluid that aids digestion and is secreted by the liver and stored in the gall bladder'. No wonder its over-production was associated with distress and depression, as anyone who has ever suffered from the acidic bite of a stomach ulcer will testify.

The theory of the four humours was an early example of biological determinism, and versions of it are still around today. But big questions hang over the theory. Does our inherited biological make up dictate our personalities, or is it the other way round? Or is it a bit of both? When a friend of mine was dying of cancer, she was accused by someone of not looking after herself, the implication being that her cancer had been self-inflicted. Unfeeling as that remark was, we do acknowledge today that there is a body-mind continuum, a feedback system that makes it hard to separate human biology from human psychology. The popularity of the mindfulness movement and other versions of self-culture testify to that, as do circular debates about the relationship between the brain and the mind.

Freud was interesting on the subject. He would not have agreed with the biological detail of the theory of humours, but he accepted the premise that human afflictions could be psychogenetic rather than purely somatic in origin. This is what he said about melancholia:

> Melancholia, the definition of which fluctuates even in descriptive psychiatry, appears in various different clinical forms; these do not seem amenable to being grouped together into a single entity, and some of them suggest somatic rather than psychogenetic diseases.[3]

Whatever line we take on it, it has to be admitted that human personality is complex, and human personalities cover a wide spectrum. And whether or not we associate it with the painful over-production of digestive acid, there *is* a type of person we usually describe as a 'moaner', someone for whom life and its normal stresses are experienced as being uniquely burdensome. I seem to have known quite a few people like this over the years. Translated in this way, for melancholics life is hard and filled with difficulty. The pressure of coping with it may even pull their mouths down into a permanent droop, so they end up looking like a version of the ancient mask of tragedy. 'Woe is me,' they complain, 'no one understands what miseries I endure.' That, I guess, was the original version of the melancholic: the person for whom life was heavy-going, the droopy-faced moaner.

But there was always a seed of something else in there as well. Not so much moaning about their own life, as seeing into the sadness and sorrow of life itself. A classic version of this understanding of melancholia is found in the epic poem the *Aeneid*, by the Roman poet Virgil (70 BCE–19 CE), which describes Aeneas's escape from the flames of ruined Troy and the long journey that brings him at last to Rome. In the passage in question, journeying Aeneas is in a Carthaginian temple gazing at a mural that depicts the deaths of some of his friends and countrymen in the battles of the Trojan War. Moved to tears at the sight, he cries out: *'En Priamus. Sunt hic etiam sua praemia laudi; sunt lacrimae rerum et mentem mortalia tangunt.'*[4] 'See, there's Priam; even here honour gets her due; there are tears at the heart of things and the fleeting nature of everything overwhelms the mind.' That captures the deepening understanding of melancholia. Melancholics are not moaners, it is just that they have a piercing awareness of the tears at the heart of things, and the sorrow and loss that characterise human history. No longer the acidic bile of the solipsistic moaner, melancholia is now understood as a sorrowing empathy for the constant defeats of the human condition. Freud would have nodded in agreement here and pointed out the close relationship between mourning and melancholy.

The correlation between melancholia and mourning seems justified by the overall picture of the two conditions. Further, the causes of both in terms of environmental influences are, where we can identify them at all, also the same. Mourning is commonly the reaction to the loss of a beloved person or an abstraction taking the place of the person, such as fatherland, freedom, an ideal and so on. In some people, whom we for this reason suspect of having a pathological disposition, melancholia appears in place of mourning.[5]

By the time of the poet John Milton (1608–74) the evolution of the understanding of melancholy had taken a definite turn in this direction. In his poems, 'L'Allegro' and 'Il Penseroso', Milton compared and contrasted the happy man with the serious or thoughtful man, or, in the typology of the four humours, the sanguine with the melancholic. Here's L'Allegro, the happy man, dismissing his gloomy opposite number by multiplying metaphors for the black bile that was supposed to provoke melancholia:

Hence loathèd Melancholy
Of Cerberus and blackest midnight born,
In Stygian cave forlorn
'Mongst horrid shapes, and shrieks, and sights
    unholy;
Find out some uncouth cell,
Where brooding Darkness spreads his jealous wings,
And the night-raven sings;
There, under ebon shades, and low-brow'd rocks,
As ragged as thy Locks,
In dark Cimmerian desert ever dwell.[6]

And here's Il Penseroso, the serious or thoughtful man, returning the favour:

Hence vain deluding joyes,
The brood of folly without father bred,
How little you bested,
Or fill the fixèd mind with all your toyes:
Dwell in some idle brain,
And fancies fond with gaudy shapes possess,
As thick and numberless
As the gay motes that people the Sun Beams,
Or likest hovering dreams
The fickle Pensioners of Morpheus' train.
But hail thou Goddess, sage and holy,
Hail divinest Melancholy . . .[7]

There has been a distinct shift in the meaning of our word. It has moved from seeing the melancholic as a depressive who is always moaning about how tough life is, to under-standing the melancholy person as thoughtful and reflective, the opposite of the pleasure-seeker who flits from sensation to sensation as if afraid to look too deeply into the tears at the heart of things. In a phrase from another poem by Eavan Boland, the melancholic has become the kind of person who knows 'how to teach a sorrow to speak'.

By the time we get to the twentieth century and the writings of Jan Morris, this is the meaning the word has. Melancholy has become a kind of grateful sadness at what life has given us but which we can never cling to, because it is constantly *passing*, disappearing into the past. Melancholics find it impossible not to keep looking back at what time has wrought as it slips away behind them like the wake of a ship. And it was because she felt the pull of melancholy with particular force when standing in her imagination on the waterfront of the city at the end of a strip of Italian territory between Slovenia and the Adriatic Sea that Jan Morris calls it her Trieste mood. This is how she describes it:

> There are moments in my life when a suggestion of Trieste is summoned so exactly into my consciousness that wherever I am I feel myself transported there . . .
>
> None of my responses to these scenes are exuberant, but they are not despondent either. I am homesick, I am thinking sad thoughts about age, doubt and disillusion, but I am not unhappy. I feel there are good people around me, and an unspecified yearning steals narcotically over me – what the Welsh call *hiraeth*. Pathos is part of it, but in a lyrical form to which I am sentimentally susceptible, and at the same time I am excited by a suggestion of sensual desire. The allure of lost consequence and faded power is seducing me, the passing of time, the passing of friends, the scrapping of great ships! The Trieste effect, I call it. It is as though I have been taken, for a brief sententious glimpse, out of time to nowhere.[8]

As I have already said, I am susceptible to this mood myself and I am conscious of it as I am writing now. In Jan Morris's words, I am pierced by the sweet sorrow of 'the passing of time' and 'the passing of friends'. Why are some of us afflicted with the compulsion to go back to places in our past that have an enduring hold on our imagination, places that soothe and hurt

us at the same time? And why is it a tendency that
afflicts so many writers? Or have I maybe got that back
to front? Is it that the insistent pressure of the melancholic mood forces some of us to become writers in
order to save as much of the past as we can from the
oblivion it hurtles towards? Is that why we go back to
places that once held meaning for us, not in hope to
recover the meaning but to revisit the place where we
once possessed it? In my case it may be to an old graveyard in a former monastery where I spent my formative
years. Or to a road up a purple hill I walked with my
mother, when I was young and she was still beside me.
Or to a road up a green hill I walked with my children,
when they were young and were still beside me. Walking
into the past like this is what the Scottish poet W.S.
Graham (1918–86) did one day on the edge of old age,
when he went up the hill behind Greenock, where he
had been born, to revisit Loch Thom.

1: Just for the sake of recovering
I walked backward from fifty-six
Quick years of age wanting to see,
And managed not to trip or stumble
To find Loch Thom and turned round
To see the stretch of my childhood
Before me. Here is the loch. The same
Long-beaked cry curls across
The heather-edges of the water held
Between the hills a boyhood's walk
Up from Greenock. It is the morning.

And I am here with my mammy's
Bramble jam scones in my pocket.
The Firth is miles and I have come
Back to find Loch Thom maybe
In this light does not recognise me.

. . .

My mother is dead. My father is dead
And all the trout I used to know
Leaping from their sad rings are dead.

3: I drop my crumbs into the shallow
Weed for the minnows and pinheads.
You see that I will have to rise
And turn round and get back where
My running age will slow for a moment
To let me on. It is a colder
Stretch of water than I remember.

The curlew's cry travelling still
Kills me fairly. In front of me
The grouse flurry and settle. GOBACK
GOBACK GOBACK FAREWELL LOCH THOM.[9]

But why do this? Why heed the call of the poet to GOBACK, GOBACK? Interrogating my own experience suggests that it is because the actual process of living is like watching a movie that can never be paused, only rewound. And only when it is over, and it is too late. Our good fortune and our tragedy are that, though we cannot stop the present to bless it as time runs on, we can go back in memory to mourn and hallow it when it is over. That is the sweet hurt poets are brilliant at capturing. We heard it in Eavan Boland's recollection of her twelve-year-old daughter.

I turned around.
I turned around.
She was gone.

And in W.S. Graham's

. . . I will have to rise
And turn round and get back where
My running age will slow for a moment
To let me on.

Freud has already reminded us that in some people melancholia appears in place of mourning.[10] But why 'in place of mourning'? Why can't we understand melancholia as itself a kind of mourning, mourning for lost time and the dead past, now only available to us through the séance of memory? Which is exactly what the writers I'll be quoting in this book do. They summon up the dear, dead past. They take us back to moments in their lives that prompt sorrow as well as a mysterious sweetness.

But, to return to an earlier question, why do writers go to all this bother? Why can't they just *be* melancholic, sense the tears at the heart of things, the passing of everything? Why do they have to *write* about it, and share their sorrow with the rest of us? Indeed, why am I bothering to anthologise their wistfulness in yet another book? To get personal: do I think the world, already drowning in words, needs to hear more from me? I was once accused by a friend of leaving no thought unpublished. An exaggeration, I thought, but I pleaded guilty, nevertheless. But why go on doing it well into my ninth decade? Is it vanity, a sense of my own significance, the conviction that I have something to say that people need to hear? I think I have found the answer to that self-accusatory question, and I'll get to it later, but because I revere him as one of the most ruthlessly honest and self-examined writers of the twentieth century, I want to look first at how George Orwell went about answering the same question. Though he doesn't say it directly, he comes close to my own earlier suggestion that it is melancholy that forces some of us to become writers in order to record the past before it is swallowed by oblivion.

In an essay he wrote in 1946, called 'Why I Write', Orwell concluded with these words:

All writers are vain, selfish and lazy, and at the very bottom of their motives there lies a mystery. Writing a book is a horrible, exhausting struggle, like a bout of some painful illness. One would never undertake such a thing if one were not driven on by some demon whom one can neither resist nor understand. For all one knows that demon is simply the same instinct that makes a baby squall for attention. And yet it is also true that one can write nothing readable unless one constantly struggles to efface one's own personality. Good prose is like a window pane. I cannot say with certainty which of my motives are the strongest, but I know which of them deserve to be followed. And looking back through my work, I see that it is invariably where I lacked a *political* purpose that I wrote lifeless books and was betrayed into purple passages, sentences without meaning, decorative adjectives and humbug generally.[11]

The endearing and reassuring thing about that passage at the end of his essay is that it seems to contradict what he had written at the start. Here's how he began:

From a very early age, perhaps the age of five or six, I knew that when I grew up I should be a writer. Between the ages of about seventeen and twenty-four I tried to abandon the idea, but I did so with the consciousness that I was outraging my true nature and that sooner or later I should have to settle down and write books . . . When I was about sixteen I suddenly discovered the joy of mere words . . . the sounds and association of words.[12]

He went on to offer what he called 'four great motives for writing'. The first was what he called 'sheer egoism'. He chose the wrong word, I think, or not quite the right word, but it was a helpful mistake and I am going to stick with it. I think he meant 'ego*tism*'. Ego*tists* have an inflated sense of their own importance and capacity to illuminate life's mysteries, allied to a compulsion to thrust their confident solutions upon the rest of us. And that is definitely a valid description of many writers. Orwell says they write 'to seem clever, to be talked about, to be remembered after death, to get your own back on grown-ups who snubbed you in childhood . . .'[13]

Ego*ists* are also preoccupied with themselves and their struggles with meaning, but this does not necessarily imply feelings of superiority. The opposite is just as likely to be true, with feelings of uncertainty and self-doubt their prevailing temper. And this may be another reason they are compelled to write. They are trying to figure things out. This seems to have been the main motive behind the compulsive diary-keeping of A.C. Benson, another man who couldn't *not* write, and continued to do it almost up to the moment he died. Benson (1862–1925) was housemaster at Eton before becoming Master of Magdalene College, Cambridge, where he died in June 1925. Interestingly, he was also a manic-depressive who, in his depressed phases, perfectly fitted the original definition of the melancholic as someone poisoned with black bile. And when he was not immobilised with despair he wrote with an almost manic intensity. He wrote many books, but today he is remembered for his diary, which, by the time of his death, amounted to five million words. David Newsome, his biographer and editor, explores his writing compulsion like this:

> Why, it may be asked, does a man take the trouble to write a diary – especially a diary of such substance as this? He may feel that his life is so important that he owes it to posterity to record his actions and impressions day by day; or that the times in which he is living, and the events he is privileged to witness, are so momentous that – granted the faculty of accurate observation and a fluent pen – he must take upon himself the task of the chronicler. He may write in order to justify a controversial life or a much-abused career; he may be so introspective and self-absorbed that he can only get to grips with his doubts and dilemmas through the medium of a *journal intime*. Or, quite simply, he may so enjoy the exercise of writing that his diary becomes a sort of personal indulgence – the satisfaction of some compulsive craving for self-analysis and self-expression.[14]

Whichever side of the divide they fall on – egotists or egoists – writers *are* self-centred creatures who are compelled to share with the rest of the world either their confident solutions to or their constant struggles with the problems of existence. I see myself in that description, hoping it classifies me as an egoist rather than an egotist, but I suspect it may be both.

Orwell goes on to offer another motive for writing:

. . . aesthetic enthusiasm. Perception of beauty in the external world, or, on the other hand, in words and their right arrangement. Pleasure of the impact of one sound on another, in the firmness of good prose or the rhythm of a good story.[15]

I recognise myself in that too. The sensual appeal of words, the pain and pleasure they impart. And I find myself in his next motive, which he called, 'Historical impulse. Desire to see things as they are, to find out true facts and store them up for the use of posterity.' His fourth motive was 'Political purpose – using the word "political" in the widest possible sense. Desire to push the world in a certain direction, to alter other people's idea of the kind of society that they should strive after . . . The opinion that art should have nothing to do with politics is itself a political attitude.' He concluded:

It can be seen how these various impulses must war against one another, and how they must fluctuate from person to person and from time to time. By nature – taking your 'nature' to be the state you have attained when you are first adult – I am a person in whom the first three motives outweigh the fourth.[16]

I can see myself in most of what Orwell has said here about writers. And something else he dropped in almost incidentally fits me as well. In making the case for authorial egoism/egotism, he says that 'the great mass of human beings are not acutely selfish. After about the age of thirty they abandon individual ambition – in many cases, indeed,

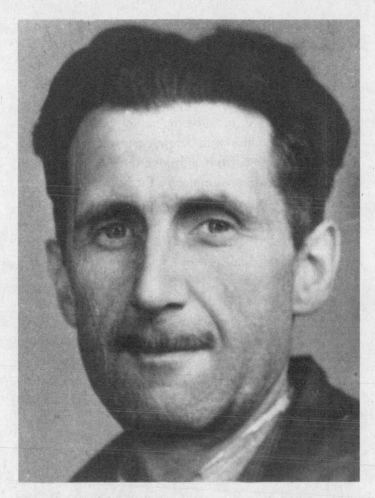

they almost abandon the sense of being individuals at all
– and live chiefly for others, or are simply smothered under
drudgery'. Society has changed significantly since he wrote
those words seventy-five years ago, but his main insight is
still valid, especially when he compared the 'great mass of
human beings' to 'the minority of gifted wilful people',

among whom he included writers, 'who are determined to live their own lives to the end'.[17]

I see myself described in these words, but why do I recognise myself with a pang of guilt rather than a simple acknowledgement of fact? Probably because, as well as the lure of the past, most of my writing has been motivated by my struggles with religion and the problem of meaning, and writers from faith communities are supposed to be exempt from or immune to the normal egotism of authors − except they're not. It is a relief now to admit that. Even to confess it. After all, it is a well-known theme in the history of religion. The American theologian Reinhold Niebuhr nailed it in a few lines:

Think of sitting Sunday after Sunday under some professional holy man who is constantly asserting his egotism by criticizing yours. I would rebel, if I were a layman. A spiritual leader who has too many illusions is useless. One who has lost his illusions about mankind and retains his illusions about himself is insufferable. Let the process of disillusionment continue until the self is included.[18]

All that admitted or confessed, I think there was a significant omission in Orwell's forensic analysis of the motivations of writers. I am wondering, hesitantly, if it was because there might have been little melancholy in his psychological make up. But whatever the reason, the important omission in his register of motives for writing is to mourn the fact that, since everything is passing away, it is owed a duty of remembrance before it disappears.

There might even be a tone of defiance to the mourning, a refusal to be reconciled to it, but its main note is a mournful recognition that all things come to an end, that every summer passes into winter and every life into death.

> November does not weep
> at the burning of the leaves
> and the pulling down of blinds.

> Only us, who know we die,
> and go to our long home
> in the inexhaustible earth.[19]

II

MOURNING

As I have just said, sometimes our mourning is marked with defiance and a refusal to be resigned to it, but mourning it remains. Here is an example from the American poet Edna St Vincent Millay (1892–1950):

I am not resigned to the shutting away of loving
    hearts in the hard ground.
So it is, and so it will be, for so it has been, time out
    of mind:
Into the darkness they go, the wise and the lovely.
    Crowned
With lilies and with laurel they go; but I am not
    resigned.

Lovers and thinkers, into the earth with you.
Be one with the dull, the indiscriminate dust.
A fragment of what you felt, of what you knew,
A formula, a phrase remains, – but the best is lost.

The answers quick and keen, the honest look, the
    laughter, the love, –

They are gone. They are gone to feed the roses.
　Elegant and curled
Is the blossom. Fragrant is the blossom. I know. But
　I do not approve.
More precious was the light in your eyes than all the
　roses in the world.

Down, down, down into the darkness of the grave
Gently they go, the beautiful, the tender, the kind;
Quietly they go, the intelligent, the witty, the brave.
I know. But I do not approve. And I am not
　resigned.[1]

Defiance is one response to all that going down into the
darkness of the grave and the fading of everything into
the past. So is hope, but it has a very different feel. Genuine
hope is tentative, wistful. There might even be a touch of
desperation in it. Wishing won't give us another life beyond
death, but who can condemn us for trying? The laureate
of this kind of longing was the English poet John Betjeman
(1906–84). Here he is raising his voice not in defiance, but
in hope:

The sky widens to Cornwall. A sense of sea
Hangs in the lichenous branches and still there's light.
The road from its tunnel of blackthorn rises free
　To a final height,

And over the west is glowing a mackerel sky
Whose opal fleece has faded to purple pink.

In this hour of the late-lit, listening evening, why
    Do my spirits sink?

The tide is high and a sleepy Atlantic sends
Exploring ripple on ripple down Polzeath shore,
And the gathering dark is full of the thought of
    friends
    I shall see no more.

Where is Anne Channel who loved this place the
    best,
With her tense blue eyes and her shopping-bag falling
    apart,
And her racy gossip and nineteen-twenty zest,
    And that warmth of heart?

Where's Roland, easing his most unwieldy car
With its load of golf-clubs, backwards into the lane?
Where Kathleen Stoke with her Sealyhams? There's
    Doom Bar;
    Bray Hill shows plain.

For this is the turn, and the well-known trees draw
    near;
On the road their pattern in moonlight fades and
    swells:
As the engine stops, from two miles off I hear
    St Minver bells.

What a host of stars in a wideness still and deep:
What a host of souls, as a motor-bike whines away

And the silver snake of the estuary curls to sleep
  In Daymer Bay.

Are they one with the Celtic saints and the years
  between?
Can they see the moonlit pools where ribbonweed
  drifts?
As I reach our hill, I am part of a sea unseen –
  And oppression lifts.[2]

It has been suggested that belief in an afterlife was
invented to answer the question asked here by Betjeman,
when he wonders what has happened to his beloved
dead:

Are they one with the Celtic saints and the years
between?
Can they see the moonlit pools where ribbonweed
drifts?

Betjeman was an attractive example of the wistful tenacity
of hope in life after death. In 1981 and 1982, a few years
before his own death, he agreed to make a series of television programmes with the producer Jonathan Stedall. In
the last programme Stedall asked him about his faith, to
which Betjeman replied:

> I hope 'The Management' is benign and in charge of
> us. I do very much hope that.
> Stedall: Hope rather than believe?
> Betjeman: Yes, certainly hope. Hope's my chief
> virtue.[3]

There is a tinge of uncertainty in the word hope that is
defiantly banished in the Christian funeral service, in the
words intoned over the body as it is lowered into the
ground:

> . . . earth to earth, ashes to ashes, dust to dust; in sure
> and certain hope of the general resurrection in the last
> day and the life of the world to come.[4]

Can hope be 'sure and certain'? It seems like a contradic-
tion to me, but whatever the answer, it is a phrase whose
denial of the absoluteness of death continues to give
comfort to millions who believe their dead have not

vanished for ever, but have 'only slipped away into the next room', as Canon Henry Scott Holland (1847–1918) expressed it in an address in St Paul's Cathedral, London, in 1910:

> Death is nothing at all.
> It does not count.
> I have only slipped away into the next room.
> Nothing has happened.[1]

But if you do not possess this faith and hope, if you think death is the absolute extinction of a life bound closely to your own, then the passing of one you love is experienced as a loss beyond any consolation.

> I am not resigned to the shutting away of loving
>   hearts in the hard ground.
> So it is, and so it will be, for so it has been, time out
>   of mind:
> Into the darkness they go, the wise and the lovely.
>   Crowned
> With lilies and with laurel they go; but I am not
>   resigned.

One of the most wrenching expressions of this refusal to be resigned to death is found in Virginia Woolf's novel *The Waves,* a challenging book to read, but one that yields riches to those who persist. In it we listen to the voices in the minds of a group of six friends, Bernard, Rhoda, Jinny, Louis, Neville and Susan, whose stories are woven through a series of soliloquies as they are carried towards what Philip Larkin called '. . . age, and then the only end of age'.[6] As well as listening to the characters talking to themselves, there are descriptive pages, all italicised, of the sea at its unceasing work encircling the globe:

The sun rose higher. Blue waves, green waves swept a quick fan over the beach, circling the spikes of sea-holly and leaving shallow pools of light here and there on the sand. A faint black rim was left behind. The rocks which had been misty and soft hardened and were marked with red clefts . . . Meanwhile the concussion of the waves breaking fell with muffled thuds, like logs falling, on the shore.[7]

The Waves is not only about the surging tide that propels us all to death, it is also about a particular death, a death that comes into a number of Virginia Woolf's books, the death of her brother, the charismatic Thoby Stephen – Percival in this novel. We never encounter Percival directly in the novel. What we get is a sense of him through his impact on the consciousness of his friends and the astonished disbelief with which they hear about his death.

'He is dead', said Neville. 'He fell. His horse tripped. He was thrown. The sails of the world have swung round and caught me on the head. All is over. The lights of the world have gone out. There stands the tree which I cannot pass.

'Oh, to crumple this telegram in my fingers – to let the light of the world flood back – to say this has not happened! But why turn one's head hither and thither? This is the truth. This is the fact. His horse stumbled;

he was thrown. The flashing trees and the white rails went up in a shower. There was a surge; a drumming in his ears. Then the blow; the world crashed; he breathed heavily. He died where he fell.

'Barns and summer days in the country, rooms where we sat – all now lie in the unreal world which is gone. My past is cut from me . . . Why try to lift my foot and mount the stair? This is where I stand; here, holding the telegram. The past, summer days and rooms where we sat, stream away like burnt paper . . . Why meet and resume? Why talk and eat and make up other combinations with other people? From this moment I am solitary. No one will know me now . . . I will not lift my foot to climb the stair. I will stand for one moment beneath the immitigable tree . . .'[8]

The Waves was published in 1931, but it is impossible to read it now without seeing it as predictive of Virginia Woolf's own death ten years later. We remember how she walked into the tidal river near her home in Sussex when the onset of another wave of madness became too much for her to bear. Before she filled her pockets with stones and drowned herself, she left for her husband, Leonard Woolf, one of the purest love letters ever written.

Dearest,
I feel certain I am going mad again. I feel we can't go through another of those terrible times. And I shan't recover this time. I begin to hear voices, and I can't concentrate. So I am doing what seems the best thing to do. You have given me the greatest possible happi-

ness. You have been in every way all that anyone could be. I don't think two people could have been happier till this terrible disease came. I can't fight any longer. I know that I am spoiling your life, that without me you could work. And you will I know. You see I can't even write this properly. I can't read. What I want to say is I owe all the happiness of my life to you. You have been entirely patient with me and incredibly good. I want to say that – everybody knows it. If anybody could have saved me it would have been you. Everything has gone from me but the certainty of your goodness. I can't go on spoiling your life any longer.

I don't think two people could have been happier than we have been.

She left this letter for Leonard, and one for her sister Vanessa, on the table in the upstairs sitting room, then:

She walked out of the garden, through the gate at the end, past the church, down to the river, and along it a little way towards the bridge at Southease . . . The river was running very fast and high – the banks of the Ouse are always bare because of the speed of the flow. She picked up a large stone from the bank, put it in her pocket, let go of her stick, and walked or jumped into the river. She could swim, but she allowed herself to be drowned.[9]

An act prophetically anticipated by Bernard on the last page of *The Waves* . . .

And in me too the wave rises. It swells; it arches its back . . . Against you I will fling myself, unvanquished and unyielding, O Death![10]

Neville's words earlier in the novel – 'the past, summer days and rooms where we sat, stream away like burnt paper' – carry an emotional charge that strengthens the idea of 'passing' as a valid way of talking not only about death, but about life itself. The past is the place into which our lives flow, but not only *our* lives, time itself: it bears us back 'ceaselessly into the past'. The phrase is the last line in F. Scott Fitzgerald's novel *The Great Gatsby,* published in 1926. There are lines in the book a few pages earlier that stun me with an even greater sense of the passingness of everything and the impossibility of holding on to any of it – except in memory and the sweet sorrow of melancholy it provokes.

One of my most vivid memories is of coming back West from prep school and later from College at Christmas time. Those who went further than Chicago would gather in the old dim Union Station at six o'clock of a December evening, with a few Chicago friends, already caught up into their own holiday gaieties, to bid them a hasty goodbye. I remember the fur coats of the girls returning from Miss This-or-That's and the chatter of frozen breath and the hands waving overhead as we caught sight of old acquaintances, and the matchings of invitations. 'Are you going to the Ordways'? the Herseys'? the Schultzes'? and the long green tickets clasped tight in our gloved hands. And last the murky

yellow cars of the Chicago, Milwaukee and St Paul
railroad looking cheerful as Christmas itself on the
tracks beside the gate.

When we pulled out into the winter night and the
real snow, our snow, began to stretch out beside us and
twinkle against the windows, and the dim lights of small
Wisconsin stations moved by . . .'[11]

Reading that, I am pierced by a precise and particular
memory of a railway journey of my own. It is the third
week in December 1950, and I am on the overnight LNER
train to Glasgow, going home from Kelham for Christmas.

I have bought a copy of *Picture Post* in Newark before boarding the train, and I have started leafing through it as the train pulls out of the station. Founded in 1938 as the clouds thickened over Europe, *Picture Post* was a brilliant example of British photojournalism that sold millions of copies every week, till new technologies finished it in 1957. It was the magazine equivalent of the newsreels we watched in cinemas during the pre-television years of the war, such as Pathé News and British Movietone News. Like these newsreels, *Picture Post* gave us photographs of the war, but it also brought glamour and sex into our drab lives, with features about movie stars and people in show-business. It was a backstage photograph from a variety show I am remembering *now*, as I flicked through the pages of *Picture Post* then. A black-and-white shot of a sad-looking showgirl bent over, rolling a silk stocking up her naked leg – and my heart lurched. And lurches again now at the memory.

I felt longing in that moment, but there was sorrow in it too. But what was the nature of that sorrow? For my own need, my melancholy lust? That, certainly. But sorrow also that the moment caught in the photograph had already been borne back into the past. It was over. Photography possesses this power of fixing the poignancy of a fleeting moment beyond any other form of art, except poetry, the best of which is itself a kind of verbal photography. This was something the poet and habitual photographer Philip Larkin understood better than most, as these verses from his poem 'Lines on a Young Lady's Photograph Album' prove.

But o, photography! as no art is,
Faithful and disappointing! that records
Dull days as dull, and hold-it smiles as frauds,
And will not censor blemishes
Like washing-lines, and Hall's Distemper boards,

But shows the cat as disinclined, and shades
A chin as doubled when it is, what grace
Your candour thus confers upon her face!
How overwhelmingly persuades
That this is a real girl in a real place,

In every sense empirically true!
Or is it just the past? Those flowers, that gate,
These misty parks and motors, lacerate
Simply by being over; you
Contract my heart by looking out of date.

Yes, true; but in the end, surely, we cry
Not only at exclusion but because
It leaves us free to cry. We know what was
Won't call on us to justify
Our grief, however hard we yowl across

The gap from eye to page. So I am left
To mourn (without a chance of consequence)
You, balanced on a bike against a fence;
To wonder if you'd spot the theft
Of this one of you bathing; to condense

In short, a past that now no one can share,
No matter whose your future; calm and dry,
It holds you like a heaven, and you lie
Unvariably lovely there,
Smaller and clearer as the years go by.[12]

What Larkin understood about photography was that it
captured the past in a way that no other art could achieve,
and broke the heart in doing so.

                    Those flowers, that gate,
These misty parks and motors, lacerate
Simply by being over; you
Contract my heart by looking out of date.

It is significant that Larkin was a photographer as well as
a poet, both arts that capture *what was* with the same heart-
breaking precision. As does great fiction. That is what the
pages at the end of *The Great Gatsby* do to me. Nick's heart
may not be broken by the end of the novel, as he is borne
back by memory into the past, but what he says lacerates
me *simply by being over*.

. . . a sharp wild brace came suddenly into the air. We
drew in deep breaths of it as we walked back from
dinner through the cold vestibules, unutterably aware
of our identity with this country for one strange hour,
before we melted indistinguishably into it again.
    That's my Middle West – not the wheat or the prairies
or the lost Swede towns, but the thrilling returning trains

of my youth, and the street lamps and sleigh bells in
the frosty dark and the shadows of holly wreaths thrown
by lighted windows on the snow. I am part of that, a
little solemn with the feel of those long winters . . .[13]

The Middle West still has those long winters but the dim
lights of those small Wisconsin stations went out ages
ago, except here in *Gatsby* where the memory of them
carries a particular type of sadness. It's their gone-ness
that catches me, and the thought of those dim, extinguished lights. It is the remembering art that breaks the
heart. It recalls the dim lights of small Wisconsin stations
and the black-and-white photographs in old magazines,
and the fugitive memories they evoke. All dead and gone,
they come alive again in these pictures and on these
pages.

Generations later we catch another glimpse of these
small Wisconsin towns not from the murky yellow cars
of the Chicago, Milwaukee and St Paul railroad, but from
a Greyhound bus.

An ordinary evening in Wisconsin
seen from a Greyhound bus – mute aisles
of merchandise the sole inhabitants
of a half-darkened Five and Ten,

the tables of the single lit café awash
with unarticulated pathos, the surface membrane
of the inadvertently transparent instant
when no one is looking: outside the town

the barns, their red gone dark with sundown,
withhold the shudder of a warped terrain –
the castle rocks above, tree-clogged ravines
already submarine with nightfall, flocks

(like dark sheep) of toehold junipers,
the lucent arms of birches: purity
without a mirror, other than a mind bound
elsewhere, to tell it how it looks.[14]

The title of that poem is significant, 'Witness'. It was written
by the American poet Amy Clampitt (1920–94) and it
captures the primary purpose of poetry: noticing, recording,
witnessing the sorrows and joys of the human condition.
Some longer poems attempt more than this, by offering
interpretations or even explanations for what befalls us as
we pass through life towards its only end, but when they
do this, they muddle their purpose and confuse their

particular usefulness. This was something W.H. Auden knew. He also knew that it was the art that was important to the rest of us, no matter the quality of the life of the artist who had produced it or through whom it had come, both themes he touched on in his poem about the death of another great poet, W.B. Yeats, who died in January 1939. It was called 'In Memory of W.B. Yeats', and this is section II:

> You were silly like us; your gift survived it all:
> The parish of rich women, physical decay,
> Yourself. Mad Ireland hurt you into poetry.
> Now Ireland has her madness and her weather
>   still,
> For poetry makes nothing happen: it survives
> In the valley of its making where executives
> Would never want to tamper, flows on south
> From ranches of isolation and the busy griefs,
> Raw towns that we believe and die in; it survives,
> A way of happening, a mouth.[15]

Poetry may make nothing happen, but what it does is *notice* and *record* what is happening to others, happening to *us*. It may not fight in the battle, but it bears witness to what is happening on the battlefield, and leaves a record for time to read. And not just great events, such as wars and the deaths of famous poets. Also, those 'inadvertently transparent' moments that illuminate the everyday, even if they are only caught from the window of a Greyhound bus on 'An ordinary evening in Wisconsin'. No: *particularly* those ordinary evenings and the pathos of their tiny revelations, their glimpses into the heroism of the unimportant and unknown. In that, they are like photographs, sudden snapshots taken at random that stop the past from being utterly lost as it recedes behind us – but lost it is, which is why we mourn its passing.

A lot of these ordinary, unimportant moments do happen during great events, such as the warring and destruction that is as constant a characteristic of human history as writing poetry. And sometimes the two become one. Sometimes the warriors are also poets, or they are warriors stung into poetry by the need to witness and the refusal to forget. They sing of war and those who fight it. As one of the greatest of them put it, they write of 'war and the pity of war', our next subject. And the greatest pity of war is that it is usually the old who do the sending into war but it is the young who do the dying.

Into the earth they go,
the young dead soldiers –
armies of them.

But they come back as flowers,
bright red flowers –
fields of them.

And as names on shining walls.

III

WARRING

Every year since the end of the First World War in 1918, at the eleventh hour of the eleventh day of the eleventh month, services of remembrance for the fallen take place in communities across Britain. Though they now incorporate remembrance of the dead in all the wars we have been fighting since 1918, the pattern of the service always contains three elements crafted into the original of 1918. A minute's silence is followed by a bugler playing the Last Post, then these four lines of poetry are read:

> They shall grow not old, as we that are left grow old:
> Age shall not weary them, nor the years condemn.
> At the going down of the sun and in the morning
> We will remember them.

Most people have heard those lines, many of us can recite them by heart, but few people know where they came from or who wrote them. It feels as if they had always been there, self-realised to fill the necessary moment.

They come, in fact, from the fourth quatrain of a poem of seven stanzas called, 'For the Fallen', written by

Laurence Binyon and published in the *Times* newspaper on 21 September 1914, only a couple of weeks into a war that killed seven million soldiers and countless civilians. And Binyon knew what he was writing about. Too old for military service himself, he had volunteered to work with the Red Cross during the Great War and was posted to the hospital at Arc-en-Barrois in the Haute-Marne, forty miles behind the lines. As well as going out in the ambulance to collect the wounded, he assisted the surgeon during the operations that inevitably followed, and afterward incinerated the arms and legs he had helped to amputate. Here's a poem he wrote about it.

Over the shadowy uplands rolling black
Into far woods, and the long road we track
Bordered with apparitions, as we pass,
Of trembling poplars and lamp-whitened grass,
A brief procession flitting like a thought
Through a brain drowsing into slumber; nought

But we awake in the solitude immense!
But hurting the vague dumbness of my sense
Are fancies wandering the night: there steals
Into my heart, like something that one feels
In darkness, the still presence of far homes
Lost in deep country, and in little rooms
The vacant bed. I touch the world of pain
That is so silent. Then I see again
Only those infinitely patient faces
In the lantern beam, beneath the night's vast spaces,
Amid the shadows and the scented dew;
And those illumined flowers, springing anew
In freshness like a smile of secrecy
From the gloom-buried earth, return to me.
The village sleeps; blank walls, and windows barred.
But lights are moving in the hushed courtyard
As we glide up to the open door. The Chief
Gives every man his order, prompt and brief.
We carry up our wounded, one by one.
The first cock crows: the morrow is begun.[1]

Who was he? Born in Lancaster in 1869, Binyon was the
modest and clever son of a Church of England vicar.
After a degree in classics at Oxford, where he won the
Newdigate Prize for Poetry and published a volume of
verse that received a rave review from Oscar Wilde, he
worked for the next forty years for the British Museum,
where he finished his career as Keeper of Prints and
Drawings. Remembered as a minor poet today – if
remembered at all – he was highly regarded by the major
poets of his time, including T.S. Eliot, whom he succeeded

as Norton Professor of Poetry at Harvard University in 1933.[2]

I came across Binyon just when I needed to, in Philip Larkin's *Oxford Book of Twentieth Century English Verse*, published in 1973. There were memories of loss and failure in my life I could not get rid of or move on from. Then, in working my way through Larkin's eccentric curation of twentieth-century poetry, I came across this:

Now is the time for the burning of the leaves.
They go to the fire; the nostril pricks with smoke
Wandering slowly into a weeping mist.
Brittle and blotched, ragged and rotten sheaves!
A flame seizes the smouldering ruin and bites
On stubborn stalks that crackle as they resist.

The last hollyhock's fallen tower is dust;
All the spices of June are a bitter reek,
All the extravagant riches spent and mean.
All burns! The reddest rose is a ghost;
Sparks whirl up, to expire in the mist: the wild
Fingers of fire are making corruption clean.

Now is the time for stripping the spirit bare,
Time for the burning of days ended and done,
Idle solace of things that have gone before:
Rootless hopes and fruitless desire are there;
Let them go to the fire with never a look behind.
The world that was ours is a world that is ours no
    more.

> They will come again, the leaf and the flower, to
>   arise
> From squalor of rottenness into the old splendour,
> And magical scents to a wondering memory
>   bring;
> The same glory, to shine upon different eyes.
> Earth cares for her own ruins, naught for ours.
> Nothing is certain, only the certain spring.[5]

I loved the whole poem, but it was the third stanza I needed to hear:

> Now is the time for stripping the spirit bare,
> Time for the burning of days ended and done,
> Idle solace of things that have gone before:
> Rootless hopes and fruitless desire are there;
> Let them go to the fire with never a look behind.
> The world that was ours is a world that is ours no
>   more.

What I did not realise at the time was that 'The Burning of the Leaves' was also a war poem, provoked, this time, not by Binyon's work collecting the wounded from the trenches of the First World War, but by watching the bombing of London in the Second. And its tone was different to 'For the Fallen'. No longer a heroic salutation of those who had given their lives for a noble cause, now there was a tragic recognition that war was a madness that had afflicted humanity since its beginning and might one day accomplish its end. There was consolation in remembering that the earth and its rhythms would survive us and might even be better off without us, like the greening and wilding of the desolation left by the nuclear accident in 1986 at Chernobyl in Ukraine, long after humans had abandoned the desolation they had created.

Earth cares for her own ruins, naught for ours.
Nothing is certain, only the certain spring.

Of course, as well as being about war and its destructions, it was about much more than that. It was about more than Binyon himself could know even as he was writing it, because poetry is greater than the intention of its makers and continues to reveal new meanings long after they are gone – 'the same glory, to shine upon different eyes'. That was why, knowing nothing about the situation that provoked it, I was able to read 'The Burning of the Leaves' thirty years later and find significance in it for my own life. There are many kinds of warfare, including conflicts in the human soul, and they have all prompted poetry that represents the human condition in all its tragedy and grace. There is also poetry that warns. That was the intention of another great war poet, Wilfred Owen. In the preface to his *Collected Poems* – which came out in 1920 a couple of years after he was killed in action on 4 November 1918, in the closing days of the war – Owen warned us:

This book is not about heroes. English poetry is not yet fit to speak of them.

Nor is it about deeds, or lands, nor anything about glory, honour, might, majesty, dominion, or power, except War.

Above all I am not concerned with Poetry.
My subject is War, and the pity of War.
The poetry is in the pity.
Yet these elegies are to this generation in no sense consolatory. They may be to the next. All a poet can do today is warn. That is why the true Poets must be truthful.[4]

Owen would have agreed with W.H. Auden in his poem written at the beginning of yet another world war, in 'September 1, 1939':

All I have is a voice
To undo the folded lie . . .[5]

It was an unfinished scrap of verse by Owen that best captured the truth of war, and the pity of war.

I saw his round mouth's crimson deepen as it fell,
    Like a Sun, in his last deep hour:
Watched the magnificent recession of farewell,
    Clouding, half gleam, half glower,
And a last splendour burn the heavens of his cheek.
    And in his eyes
The cold stars lighting, very old and bleak,
    In different skies.[6]

In writing truthful poetry about war, and the pity of war, Wilfred Owen and Laurence Binyon belonged in a long succession of poets, the greatest of whom was Homer, author of the epic of the Trojan Wars, the *Iliad*. In the early years of the Second World War, while Binyon was watching the bombing of London that prompted 'The Burning of the Leaves', and two years before her own death in 1943, the French philosopher and theologian Simone Weil composed a meditation on the *Iliad*. She subtitled it *The Poem of Force,* and in the opening paragraphs she tells us that the true subject of the *Iliad* – as of all war – is *force*. She writes:

> The true hero, the true subject, the centre of the *Iliad* is force. Force employed by man, force that enslaves man, force before which man's flesh shrinks away . . . For those dreamers who considered that force, thanks to progress, would soon be a thing of the past, the *Iliad* could appear as an historical document; for others, whose powers of recognition are more acute and who perceive force, today as yesterday, at the very centre of human history, the *Iliad* is the purest and loveliest of mirrors.
>
> To define force – it is that *x* that turns anybody who is subjected to it into a *thing*. Exercised to the limit, it turns man into a thing in the most literal sense: it makes a corpse out of him. Somebody was here, and the next minute there is nobody here at all; this is a spectacle the *Iliad* never wearies of showing us.[7]

How can a poem about war, a poem that never wearies of showing us men being turned into corpses, be 'the purest and loveliest of mirrors'? We know poets reflect us and our actions back to us, but how can a poem that mirrors the madness of war be pure and lovely? Because, in Owen's phrase, it is 'truthful', or, in Auden's phrase,

it works 'To undo the folded lie'. And because it is
truthful, it shows us death turning us into things.
'Somebody was here, and the next minute there is nobody
here at all'. Death usually has to wait to achieve that
transformation. It usually collects us when we are old
and weak and ugly. But in war it does not have to wait.
In war it gets us when we are young and strong and
handsome. And there is beauty as well as sorrow in that
spectacle, the beauty of the given-away life, the life sacri-
ficed for others. As A.E. Housman described it:

> Here dead we lie because we did not choose
> To live and shame the land from which we sprung.
> Life, to be sure, is nothing much to lose;
> But young men think it is, and we were young.[8]

That is why, on Armistice Day, the silence followed by the
lament of the bagpipes over the killing fields where now
only poppies grow still touches our hearts with its terrible
beauty. This is a strong theme in Scottish writing. Nowhere
is it more poignantly expressed than in Scotland's favourite
novel, the prose-poem *Sunset Song* written by Lewis Grassic
Gibbon in 1932.

It all happens in Kinraddie, an estate without a laird
that has fallen on hard times, lying in the Howe o' the
Mearns on the road from Stonehaven to Laurencekirk in
Aberdeenshire. It is the dying years of Queen Victoria's
reign and the land runs in the old ways of horse and
plough, mill and kirk. Up past Peesie's Knapp, sited below
the blue loch and the ancient standing stones, lies the
croft of Blawearie, coarse land and hard to work, 'out

of the world', as they say, 'and into Blawearie'. Into it come the Guthries: grim, tormented, lustful John and his wife and their children, the sons, Will, Dod and Alec, and the daughter, Chris, whose story it is. Chris would hear her father cry in agony at night as he went with her mother:

> One night they heard her cry to John Guthrie *Four of a family's fine; there'll be no more.* And father thundered at her, that way he had *Fine? We'll have what God in His mercy may send to us, woman. See you to that* . . . He wouldn't do anything against God's will, would father, and sure as anything God followed up Alec with the twins, born seven years later. Mother went about with a queer look on her face before they came, she lost that sweet blitheness that was hers, and once she said to father when he spoke of arranging a doctor and things, *Don't worry about that. No doubt your friend Jehovah will see to it all.* Father seemed to freeze up then, his face grew black, he said never a word, and Chris had wondered at that . . . But then . . . the twins were born and mother had as awful a time as she'd always had.[9]

Refusing to bring more children into the world to satisfy her husband's sexual needs and appease his angry god, Chris's mother poisons herself and her young twins. Will leaves and the boys are taken in by Guthrie's sister and her husband. Chris is now alone with her father, till his death releases them both from his anger and lust, and she follows his coffin to the graveyard in Kinraddie:

Chris walked free and uncaring – soon as the burial was over she'd be free as never in her life she'd been – she lifted her face to the blow of the wet September wind and the world that was free to her. Then it was that she saw Ewan Tavendale walked beside her – he glanced down just then and straight and fair up into his eyes she looked – she nearly stumbled in the slow walk because of that looking.

They marry, have a son named for his father, and run the croft at Blawearie together. Then come the horrors of the Great War in which Kinraddie is not spared. Four local men are killed in the conflict, including Ewan himself – shot for desertion. The war over, Kinraddie gathers to hear its new young minister, Robert Colquhoun, who had himself fought in the trenches, dedicate the memorial to Kinraddie's fallen.

And then, with the night waiting out by on Blawearie brae, and the sun just verging the coarse hills, the minister began to speak again, his short hair blowing in the wind that had come, his voice not decent and a kirk-like bumble, but ringing out over the loch:

FOR I WILL GIVE YOU THE MORNING STAR

In the sunset of an age and an epoch we may write that for epitaph of the men who were of it. They went quiet and brave from the lands they loved, though seldom of that love might they speak – it was not in them to tell in words of the earth that moved and lived and abided – their life and enduring love.

And who knows at the last what memories of it were with them – the springs and the winters of this land and all the sounds and scents of it that had once been theirs – deep, and a passion of their blood and spirit – those four who died in France. With them we may say there died a thing older than themselves – these were the Last of the Peasants, the last of the Old Scots folk.

A new generation comes up that will know them not, except as a memory in a song – they pass with the things that seemed good to them, with loves and desires that grow dim and alien in the days to be. It was the old Scotland that perished then – and we may believe that never again will the old speech and the old songs, the old curses and the old benedictions, rise but with alien effort to our lips. The last of the peasants – those four that you knew – took that with them to the darkness and the quietness of the places where they sleep.

And the land changes – their parks and their steadings are a desolation where the sheep are pastured – we are told that great machines come soon to till the land, and the great herds come to feed on it – the crofter is gone, the man with the house and the steading of his own – and the land closer to his heart than the flesh of his body. Nothing, it has been said, is true but change, nothing abides – and here in Kinraddie where we watch the building of those little prides and those little fortunes on the ruins of the little farms – we must give heed that these also do not abide – that a new spirit shall come to the land with the greater herd and the great machines. For greed of place and possession and great estate, those four had little heed – the kindness of friends and the warmth of toil and the peace of rest – they asked no more from God or man, and no less would they endure.

So, lest we shame them, let us believe that the new oppressions and foolish greeds are no more than mists that pass. They died for a world that is past, these men — but they did not die for this that we seem to inherit. Beyond it and us there shines a greater hope and a newer world — undreamt when these four died. But need we doubt which side the battle they would range themselves did they live today — need we doubt the answer they cry to us even now — the four of them — from the places of the sunset?

And then . . . the Highlandman McIvor tuned up his pipes and began to step slow round the stone circle by Blawearie Loch, slow and quiet, and folk watched him, the dark was near, it lifted your hair and was eerie and uncanny, the *Flowers of the Forest* as he played it:

it rose and rose and wept and cried, that crying for the men that fell in battle . . .[10]

'The Flowers of the Forest' is the lament of the young women of Scotland at the killing of their king and the flower of Scottish manhood by the English at the Battle of Flodden on 9 September 1513:

> I've heard them lilting at our ewe-milking,
>> Lasses a' lilting before dawn o' day;
> But now they are moaning on ilka green loaning,
>> The Flooers o' the Forest are a' wede away.
>
> Dool and wae for the order sent oor lads tae the
>> Border!
>> The English for ance, by guile wan the day,
> The Flooers o' the Forest, that fought aye the
>> foremost,
>> The pride o' oor land lie cauld in the clay.[11]

Strangely, it was the song Chris had sung at her own wedding feast.

> . . . it came on Chris how strange was the sadness of Scotland's singing, made for the sadness of the land and sky in dark autumn evenings, the crying of men and women of the land who had seen their lives and loves sink away in the years, things wept for beside the sheep-buchts, remembered at night and in twilight. The gladness and kindness had passed, lived and forgotten, it was Scotland of the mist and rain and the crying sea that made the songs.[12]

Even after her happy marriage to the Rev. Robert Colquhoun, Chris's melancholy never leaves her. The passing of the seasons. The sinking away of the years. The passingness of everything. In *Cloud Howe*, the second volume in Gibbon's trilogy, she wonders:

> In a ten years' time what things might have been? She might stand on this hill, she might rot in a grave, it would matter nothing, the world would go on, young Ewan dead as his father was dead, or hither and borne, far from Kinraddie: oh, once she had seen in these parks, she remembered, the truth, and the only truth that there was, that only the sky and the seasons endured, slow in their change, the cry of the rain, the whistle of the whins on a winter night under the sailing edge of the moon –
>
> And suddenly, daft-like, she found herself weep, quiet, she thought that she made no noise, but Robert knew, and his arms came round her.
>
> *It was Ewan? Oh, Chris, he won't grudge you me!*
>
> Ewan? It was Time himself she had seen, haunting their tracks with unstaying feet.'[13]

The best reason for being grateful to writers like Gibbon is that they name the terminal nature of our incurable disease, mortality. It is also why we can find a terrible beauty in war and the sacrifices it demands. And it is why some of us admire warriors though we hate war. Warriors have chosen a calling that requires them to give up their young lives for others, while we shiver at the thought of letting our old lives slip away from us. We may find it impossible to admire those in power who send the young to war. Indeed, our admiration for warriors only increases, because we know soldiers often despise those whose signature on a paper orders them to march towards the guns, but they go anyway – have always gone, and keep on going. Wilfred Owen was an example of this noble contempt of the young warrior for the old men in wood-panelled government offices who send them to their deaths. He recognised it as an ancient archetype, as old as the Bible.

So Abram rose, and clave the wood, and went,
And took the fire with him, and a knife.
And as they sojourned both of them together,
Isaac the first-born spake and said, My Father,
Behold the preparations, fire and iron,
But where the lamb for this burnt-offering?
Then Abram bound the youth with belts and straps,
And builded parapets and trenches there,
And stretchèd forth the knife to slay his son.
When lo! an angel called him out of heaven,
Saying, Lay not thy hand upon the lad,
Neither do anything to him. Behold,
A ram, caught in a thicket by its horns;
Offer the Ram of Pride instead of him.

But the old man would not so, but slew his son,
And half the seed of Europe, one by one.[14]

In November 1915, as the slaughter of the Great War was intensifying, the novelist D.H. Lawrence likened it not to the burning but to the falling of the leaves. In a letter to his friend Lady Cynthia Asquith, written from Garsington Manor, Oxfordshire, Lawrence wrote:

> When I drive across this country, with the autumn falling and rustling to pieces, I am so sad, for my country, for this great wave of civilisation, 200 years, which is now collapsing, that it is hard to live. So much beauty and pathos of old things passing away and no new things coming: this house of the Ottolines – It is England – my God, it breaks my soul – this England, these shafted windows, the elm-trees, the blue distance – the past, the great past, crumbling down, breaking down, not under the force of the coming buds, but under the weight of many exhausted, lovely yellow leaves, that drift over the lawn and over the pond, like the soldiers, passing away into winter and the darkness of winter – no, I can't bear it. For the winter stretches ahead, where all vision is lost and all memory dies out.[15]

The war Lawrence was mourning may have been the most destructive in history but it was certainly not the last. Old men go on signing pieces of paper that send young men and women to death. A modern example comes from the waste of the Vietnam War, in which 58,000 young American soldiers were killed. One of them was called Paul Castle.

> The last time I saw Paul Castle
> it was printed in gold on the wall
> above the showers in the boys'

locker room, next to the school
record for the mile. I don't recall
his time, but the year was 1968
and I can look across the infield
of memory to see him on the track,
legs flashing, body bending slightly
beyond the pack of runners at his back.

He couldn't spare a word for me,
two years younger, junior varsity,
and hardly worth the waste of breath.
He owned the hallways, a cool blonde
at his side, and aimed his interests
further down the line than we could guess.

Now, reading the name again,
I see us standing in the showers,
naked kids beneath his larger,
comprehensive force—the ones who trail
obscurely, in the wake of the swift,
like my shadow on this gleaming wall.[16]

'The gleaming wall' the poet is describing is the Vietnam
Veterans Memorial in Washington, DC, perhaps the most
moving war memorial in the world. It was opened on 13
November 1982, in the presence of more than 150,000
people.

Wheelchairs, fatigues, old Army jackets and a sea of
decorations followed the brass parade toward the park
between the Lincoln Memorial and the Washington

Monument. After the sundry speeches, when the fences guarding the memorial finally came down, there was a prolonged, uneasy silence as people surveyed the wall, approached it, touched it, walked along it, searched it for the names of fallen kin or comrades. One by one veterans began to break down. Strangers embraced, weeping in each other's arms. Mothers, fathers, wives, daughters, sons, relatives, and friends of the dead also broke down, and before long the scene of spontaneous grief moved reporters and broadcasters to tears as well.[17]

Since that day the Vietnam Veterans Memorial has become the most visited monument in the United States. Part of its power has to do with the unresolved tensions associated with the Vietnam War, but Robert Pogue Harrison believes there is also something symbolic about

. . . the solemn gravity of the wall – the encrypted presence of the dead – which seems to turn the deaths of those memorialised into a stubborn question. The silence with which it responds to this question gives the wall's inscribed black granite panels an almost over-whelming power of withholding. The irresistible need many visitors feel to touch a chiselled name, kiss it, talk to it, offer it flowers or gifts, leave it notes or letters, is evidence enough of the dead's private presence in the stone – a presence at once given and denied.[18]

Great poetry has the power to express in words what war memorials express in marble. And of this capacity to represent 'the encrypted presence of the dead', the *Iliad*, to repeat Simone Weil's words, is 'the purest and loveliest of mirrors'. And one of the truths they remind us of is that one day we too must die. It is a message underlined in a passage in George Steiner's memoir, *Errata*, where he describes his father reading to him a passage from Robert Fagles's translation of Homer's great epic. Maddened by the death of his friend Patroclus, Achilles is butchering fleeing Trojans when Lycaon crosses his path. Achilles had captured and sold Lycaon into slavery, but he has returned to help defend his father's city and sees Achilles storming towards him. Steiner reads what happens next:

. . . He ducked, ran under the hurl
And seized Achilles' knees as the spear shot past his
   back

and stuck in the earth, still starved for human flesh.
And begging now, one hand clutching Achilles'
    knees,
the other gripping the spear, holding for dear life,
Lycaon burst out with a winging prayer: 'Achilles!
I grasp your knees – respect me, show me mercy!
I am your suppliant, Prince, you must respect me!
And it's just twelve days that I've been home in Troy
    – all I've suffered!
But now again some murderous fate has placed me in
    your hands, your prisoner twice over – Father
    Zeus must hate me, giving me back to you! Ah, to
    a short life you bore me, mother, mother . . .
Listen, this too, take it to heart, I beg you –
don't kill me! I'm not from the same womb as
    Hector,
Hector who killed your friend, your strong, *gentle*
    friend!'

Steiner tells us that his father took up the original Greek
text and, placing his son's finger at the place, translated
what came next from the mouth of Achilles:

'Come, friend, you too must die. Why moan about it
    so?
Even Patroclus died, a far, far better man than you.
And look, you see how handsome and powerful I
    am?
The son of a great man, the mother who gave me
    life
a deathless goddess. But even for me, I tell you,

death and the strong force of fate are waiting.
There will come a dawn or sunset or high noon
when a man will take my life in battle too –
flinging a spear perhaps
or whipping a deadly arrow of his bow.'
Whereupon, Achilles slaughters the kneeling Lycaon.

Steiner continues, 'I recall graphically the rush of wonder, of a child's consciousness troubled and uncertainly ripened, by that single word "friend" in the midst of the death-sentence: "Come, friend, you too must die." And by the enormity, so far as I could gauge it, of the question: "Why moan about it so?"'[19] Those of us who do not even want to *think* about dying blink in amazement at that question. The poets of war insist we think about it. And face the truth: *Come friend, you too must die.*

But it is not just the living who are destroyed by war. The cities and civilisations we have created get ruined as well, flattened like Troy in Homer or like Aleppo and Palmyra in today's war in Syria. Yet the dead heroes and the shattered cities they defended live on in the art of the poets who bear witness to the force that turns us and everything we have created into dust.

Only those who have died are ours, only what we
    have lost is ours.
Ilium vanished, yet Ilium lives in Homer's verses.[20]

What I had not realised when I first came across Laurence Binyon's 'The Burning of the Leaves' was that it wasn't just a single poem. Written in 1941, it was one of five linked but separate poems, first published in *Horizon,* the legendary magazine edited by Cyril Connolly.[21] As it moves through its five sequences, it becomes clear that this is more than a bonfire of garden rubbish. This is an air-raid.

> What are they burning, what are they burning,
> Heaping and burning in a thunder-gloom?
> Rubbish of the old world, dead things, merely names,
> Truth, justice, love, beauty, the human smile,
> All flung to the flames![22]

An air-raid! And a metaphor, because in poetry nothing is ever only one thing. Here is the second poem in the sequence of five. About a deserted theatre. And much more.

> Never was anything so deserted
> As this dim theatre
> Now, when in passive grayness the remote
> Morning is here,
> Daunting the wintry glitter of the pale,
> Half-lit chandelier.

> Never was anything disenchanted
> As this silence!
> Gleams of soiled gilding on curved balconies
> Empty; immense
> Dead crimson curtain, tasselled with its old
> And staled pretence.

Nothing is heard but a shuffling and knocking
Of mop and mat,
Where dustily two charwomen exchange
Leisurely chat.
Stretching and settling to voluptuous sleep
Curls a cat.

The voices are gone, the voices
That laughed and cried.
It is as if the whole marvel of the world
Had blankly died,
Exposed, inert as a drowned body left
By the ebb of the tide.

Beautiful as water, beautiful as fire,
The voices came,
Made the eyes to open and the ears to hear,
The hand to lie intent and motionless,
The heart to flame,
The radiance of reality was there,
Splendour and shame.

Slowly an arm dropped, and an empire
    fell.
We saw, we knew.
A head was lifted, and a soul was freed.
Abysses opened into heaven and hell.
We heard, we drew
Into our thrilled veins courage of the truth
That searches us through.

But the voices are all departed,
The vision dull.
Daylight disconsolately enters
Only to annul.
The vast space is hollow and empty
As a skull.[25]

'. . . hollow and empty as a skull' – because it is more than young warriors we destroy. It is civilisation itself.

Civilisation defends us against nature,
    Freud told us;
        that's why we resent it.

We long for the time,
    before restraint,
        when we did what we wanted.

Nietzsche too was homesick
    for the warriors,
        whose will was law,

who created deserts,
    and called it peace,
        the peace of desolation.

We make our deserts too,
    faster than they did,
        pouring fire from the air.

IV

RUINING

It probably isn't how Shelley wanted us to interpret his famous poem. He almost certainly saw it as a parable of the transience of political power, which usually ends in failure and often ends in disgrace.

> My name is Ozymandias, king of kings:
> Look on my works, ye mighty, and despair!

We've heard that boast many times down the years. You only have to delete the name Ozymandias and fill in the blank from any period in history to get the message. It is the obvious way to read his poem: the proud boasts of power all fail in the end. But poetry, like scripture, can be read in many ways, so I want to give Shelley's poem another meaning. Because it is not only power that passes. The architecture of power passes too. Its forts and fortresses fall into ruin. And not just the architecture of power. The architecture of faith also crumbles, its temples turn to dust. It is a melancholy fact that what our creative genius prompts us to build, our destructive genius compels us to destroy. That is why the earth is strewn with ruins.

Round the decay
Of that colossal wreck, boundless and bare
The lone and level sands stretch far away.

Here's the whole poem:

I met a traveller from an antique land
Who said: Two vast and trunkless legs of stone
Stand in the desert . . . Near them, on the sand,
Half sunk, a shattered visage lies, whose frown,
And wrinkled lip, and sneer of cold command,
Tell that its sculptor well those passions read
Which yet survive, stamped on these lifeless things,
The hand that mocked them, and the heart that fed;
And on the pedestal, these words appear:
My name is Ozymandias, king of kings:
Look on my works, ye mighty, and despair!
Nothing beside remains. Round the decay

Of that colossal wreck, boundless and bare
The lone and level sands stretch far away.[1]

Reading about 'that colossal wreck' my imagination
summons other images of destruction from recent history,
especially the bombing of the ancient cities of Syria during
the civil war, which, at the time of writing, has been raging
for ten years. Going back to my own childhood, I can
remember my father taking me out into the street in
Alexandria in March 1941 to see the sky blazing red, miles
away over Clydebank the night it was blitzed, and telling
me never to forget the sight. Next day the bombed-out
families of Clydebank came to our town for refuge, and
my father brought a couple and their daughter home to
stay with us in our two rooms in Bridge Street. How could
I forget?

Over the centuries too many cities have endured
Shelley's epic of glory and dereliction; Binyon's 1941 lament
over bombed-out London is a vivid example. But the
archetypal ruined city has to be Jerusalem, the sacred place
that has been fought over for centuries and is still contested
today.

> O Jerusalem, Jerusalem, killing the prophets and stoning
> those who are sent to you! How often would I have
> gathered your children together as a hen gathers her
> brood under her wings, and you would not! Behold
> your house is forsaken and desolate.[2]

In these verses Matthew was lamenting the destruction
of Jerusalem by the Romans in 70 CE, but that was only
one incident in a long record that shows little sign of
ending. It is almost as if this ancient city on a hill had
been established by the Cosmic Tragedian as a symbol of
humanity's passion for creating beauty and compulsively
destroying the beauty it had created. The Bible has a whole
book of poems mourning Jerusalem's derelictions. Called
the Book of Lamentations, it mourns the destruction of
Jerusalem in 587 BCE by the Assyrians, one in a long line
of desecrators.

> How lonely sits the city
>   that was full of people!
> How like a widow has she become,
>   she that was great among the nations!
> She that was a princess among the cities
>   has become a vassal.

She weeps bitterly in the night,
    tears on her cheeks;
among all her lovers
    she has none to comfort her;
all her friends have dealt
    treacherously with her,
they have become her enemies.[3]

And on it goes – Jerusalem, the tragic symbol for all our loves and hatreds. Twenty years ago, I spent a December evening in that ancient city with the Israeli poet Yehuda Amichai, reflecting on some of these themes. One of his poems captured the tragic consequences of Jerusalem's symbolic status among the feuding religions of Abraham.

The air over Jerusalem is saturated with prayers and
    dreams
like the air over industrial cities.
It's hard to breathe.[4]

As well as giving us the kind of spiritual emphysema that damages our souls, religion at its worst can also license us to kill each other. That wise old atheist philosopher Lucretius observed thousands of years ago that there was nothing like religion for persuading humans to do evil things to each other: *tantum religio potuit suadere malorum.* Nothing, that is, except politics, the other great engine of human self-destruction. Down the centuries Jerusalem has felt the full pressure of both.

Is it nothing to you, all you who pass by?
  Look and see
if there is any sorrow like my sorrow
  which was brought upon me,
which the Lord inflicted
  on the day of his fierce anger.⁵

The destructions of Jerusalem are symbolic of humanity's addiction to violence, whether provoked by religion or politics. It is a melancholy fact that most of the ruins that litter the earth are the result of that addiction and the warfare it provokes – but not all. As well as being the most violent and self-destructive animals on the planet, humans are also the most creative and constructive. The paradox is that our restless creativity becomes the other great engine of destruction and ruination. It constantly compels us to change styles and technologies, to experiment with the new and to throw away the old. And this inventive faithlessness makes its own ruins, a paradox perfectly expressed in a meditation by Thomas Cole in 1838 called 'The Architect's Dream'.

Once upon a time an architect had a dream. The curtain of his bourgeois parlour was rent, and he found himself reclining on top of a colossal column overlooking a great port. On a nearby hill, the spire of a Gothic cathedral rose above pointed cypresses in a dark wood; on the other side of the river, a Corinthian rotunda and the brick arches of a Roman aqueduct were bathed in golden light. The aqueduct had been built on top of a Grecian colonnade, in front of which a procession led from the waterside to an elaborate Ionic shrine. Further away the form of a Doric temple crouched beneath an Egyptian palace, and behind them all, veiled in haze and a wisp of cloud, was the Great Pyramid.

It was a moment of absolute stillness. A perspective in time had become a perspective in space, as the past receded in an orderly fashion, style by style, from the parlour curtain of the present all the way back to the horizon of antiquity. The Dark Ages partially obscured classical splendour; Roman magnificence was built on the foundation of Grecian reason; the glory that was Greece lay in the shadow of the Ur architecture of Egypt. The array of buildings formed an architectural canon, each example dispensing inspiration, advice, and warning to the architect from the golden treasury of history.

All the great buildings of the past had been resurrected in a monumental day of rapture. Everything had been made new, and neither weather nor war nor wandering taste had scarred the scene. Everything was fixed just as it had been intended to be: each building was a masterpiece, a work of art, a piece of frozen music, unspoiled by compromise, error, or disappointment. There was nothing that could be added or taken away except for the worse. Each building was beautiful, its form and function held in perfect balance.

The scene was what architecture was, and is, and should be. But just before he awoke, the architect realised that he was dreaming, and he recalled the words of Prospero renouncing his conjured dominion at the end of *The Tempest*:

The cloud-capp'd towers, the gorgeous palaces,
The solemn temples, the great globe itself,
Yea, all which it inherit, shall dissolve,
And, like this insubstantial pageant faded,
Leave not a rack behind: We are such stuff
As dreams are made on, and our little life
Is rounded with a sleep.[6]

Thomas Cole's dream fills me with admiration for what our genius has built. It also fills me with sorrow over what it forces us to forsake. Behind the varieties of our architectures are the beliefs and philosophies they were created to celebrate. And they too are abandoned in our propulsive rush through time. It is all emblemised for me by a discarded church I pass as I walk the streets of Edinburgh.

In the eighteenth century, Edinburgh pushed itself north over Princes Street into the New Town to house the city's bourgeoisie far away from the noisy and fetid overcrowding of the Old Town in the Royal Mile. In the nineteenth century, it started pushing itself west to house a very different population. It built streets of solid tenements on both sides of the Union Canal in Fountainbridge – named after 'a well of sweet water' in the area – to house workers in the rubber and brewing industries that were growing in the district. The fashionable West End congregation of St John's Princes Street decided to create a mission to cater for their spiritual needs by building a little church for them, but where could they find to build it in such a crowded area? They chose an unusual place, down a pend behind a row of tenements at the point where the Viewforth Bridge crossed the canal. They decided to call it St Kentigern's, after a popular seventh-century Scottish saint, and they invited the architect John More Dick Peddie to design it.

He created a sweet and simple round-arched church, with a nave, a single aisle and a narthex, and in 1897 its life began. As an active congregation it endured for only forty-four years and was closed in 1941. Since then it has been variously used as a garage and a warehouse. Now it sits solitary; a tiny, abandoned Jerusalem.

Is it nothing to you, all you who pass by?
    Look and see
if there is any sorrow like my sorrow
    which was brought upon me . . .

It is far from nothing to me, as I pass by. It breaks my heart to see it, another mute witness to the promiscuous way we create beauty then discard it. One day this melancholy vision prompted me to go back into my own past to remember other ruins. Not, like W.S. Graham's pilgrimage to Loch Thom, to the hills and lochs of my boyhood. It was a return to the streets I walked as a young man in Glasgow's Gorbals in the 1960s, streets that were being torn down as I walked them, in pursuit of another architect's dream.

Maybe it is because I was born in one that I have always loved tenements, Scotland's dominant domestic architectural idiom, and one that defined the cityscape of Glasgow till the planners took their wrecking balls to it in the 1960s. The tenement is a classless type of architecture that can range from a single room right up to grand apartments of seven or eight rooms. Tenement construction increased in Glasgow by 600 per cent between 1862 and 1872. Around 21,000 tenement flats were built between 1872 and 1876, a surge that continued till 1900. On each of the floors of the standard working-class tenement, a single room – known as a 'single-end' – was sandwiched between two two-room flats. Few of them had lavatories or hot water, though later models had a shared WC on each landing. Middle-class flats were larger, at least three rooms, and some of them were spacious. These streets of grey and red sandstone tenements seemed organic to the landscape and climate of this northern nation. Even the cheaper ones were built to last, and they all looked as though they belonged where they stood, and knew it. Their four-storied blocks, never higher than the width of the street, were built with drying greens and ash pits out the back.

M'ASLIN STREET, GLASGOW (Looking West).

Many Scottish memoirs feature life in streets like these. The actor Sean Connery was born and grew up in a tenement like this in Fountainbridge in Edinburgh. The tenement is still a subject for Scottish artists, the most iconic being *Windows in the West* by Avril Paton, which shows life behind the glowing windows of a snow-topped tenement in Glasgow's West End, where they built a solid and enduring version of this Scottish classic.

What happened to turn so many of Scotland's solid tenements into slums? It is worth offering as a general truth that it is the poor who are forced to bear most of the burden of humanity's revolutionary history. 'The Architect's Dream' reminded us that we are the most restless and discontented species on earth. Our powerful intellects invent new products and new ways of making them. Powerful groups exploit their discoveries, becoming wealthy in the process, and they overturn the existing economic institutions. And it is always the poor who pay the price for this progress. You don't have to be a Marxist to acknowledge that what Marx called pauperism is an inevitable effect of humanity's electric restlessness. He said it was part of the incidental expenses of capitalist production, the price that had to be paid for progress. The cruelty of this law has been etched on the faces of the dispossessed from the enclosure acts, through the industrial revolution and its death throes at the end of the twentieth century, to the impact of the cyber revolution in our own day. We can admire the ferocious beauty of it all, just as we thrill when a lion brings down the weakest gazelle in the herd and drags it to its inevitable death. It is possible to understand how it works, even accept the inevitability of it all, and still be grieved by it.

And it does not end there. Something else comes along to complete the alienation. It is the way the world runs, and there's no changing it, we tell ourselves. But the consequences of our addiction to change appal even those who profit from it, so they figure out ways to modify the harshness of its impact on the poor. We know that we will never quench our passion for change and destruction, so we try to quieten our conscience by planting daffodils amid the ruins we create. Ashamed of what we have done to the poor, we assuage our consciences by trying to engineer new lives for them – without bothering to ask them what they think of our plans for them. Having torn off their garments, we insist on covering them in uniforms we ourselves have run up for them. The effect of this double whammy was clear in the history of Gorbals.

The area was completely tenemented by 1900, the later generation of buildings following the classic working-class model I have already described. In the nineteenth century the arrival of the suburban railway system started the flight of the middle classes from the area to the outskirts of the city, but the population of the district was constantly increased by new arrivals, particularly by two immigrant groups, the traces of whose presence were still very clear when I lived here in the 1960s. From Ireland, during the potato famine between 1846 and 1850, came thousands of refugees fleeing starvation and intent on finding jobs in a city that was being rapidly industrialised. Now fully integrated into the Scottish demographic mix, Irish Catholics were not welcomed by Scottish Protestants when they first arrived, and had to protect themselves against prejudice and persecution by defensive alliances that kept them isolated in their own communities, with their own religion and culture, until well into the twentieth century. The rivalry between Rangers and Celtic football clubs is the toxic residue of that turbulent period. Also into Gorbals Jewish refugees came from Europe, fleeing the pogroms of Russia and the growing menace of German fascism. By 1950 the population was over 50,000, and in its last decade of life, the 1960s, Gorbals made room for migrants from the Indian sub-continent. I remember being impressed by their industry, as they took over small shops and started cash-and-carry businesses in the area. This long period of social churn resulted in a teeming and turbulent community that knew much about violence and sorrow. It also had a fierce energy, and its people had a famous pride in their ability to survive.

It was what came after the Second World War that blew the community apart. Glasgow's housing stock was in a terrible state by the end of the war. An official survey established that 98,000 houses in the city were technically unfit for human habitation. No one doubted that something radical had to be done to improve the city's housing. But what the planners decided to do was brutal. In the intervening half century since their big plan, most of it has been reversed, but at a cost. Many of us argued at the time that the best response to the housing crisis was to modernise and rehabilitate the existing stock. We pointed out that Glasgow's traditional tenements had been a good solution to population density at the time they were built, so why not keep the stair system, but reduce the number of flats on each landing? Had they been consulted, that is what the natives themselves would have gone for, but social engineers are famous for their indifference to the views of the subjects of their experiments. No one bothered to ask.

They opted for what they called comprehensive redevelopment. As the term suggests, this meant the complete flattening of a district and the erection of an entirely new street and housing pattern. It was an astonishingly violent concept and once a district was sentenced to it a deadly blight descended on it. It was putting a whole neighbourhood on death row for decades before muscling it onto the electric chair. Edwin Morgan, Glasgow's Poet Laureate or Makar, caught the misery of it.

A mean wind wanders through the backcourt trash.
Hackles on puddles rise, old mattresses
puff briefly and subside. Play-fortresses
of brick and bric-a-brac spill out some ash.
Four storeys have no windows left to smash,
but in the fifth a chipped sill buttresses

mother and daughter the last mistresses
of that black block condemned to stand, not crash.
Around them the cracks deepen, the rats crawl.
The kettle whimpers on a crazy hob.
Roses of mould grow from ceiling to wall.
The man lies late since he has lost his job,
smokes on one elbow, letting his coughs fall
thinly into an air too poor to rob.[7]

Had some organising genius been able to magic the scheme
into immediate realisation it might have worked, but it was
piecemeal and sporadic in its approach. Stumps of decaying
tenements were left standing in the rubble of partial demo-
lition, pierced by twenty-storey tower blocks erected to
contain some of the displaced population. Basil Spence was
knighted for his contribution to the desecration. Sky-
scrapers can be good places to live, if the towers are carefully
and safely designed, as they usually are for the wealthy in
places like Manhattan. The poor design and low-quality
construction of the Gorbals towers led to serious health
problems for many of the inmates. With the black humour
that characterised the area, it was said of Spence's Queen
Elizabeth arcade that if you sneezed at the entrance you
would have pneumonia by the time you got to the other end.

Old Gorbals flicked dust from his sleeve,
      sighed a bit and swore a bit,
      made for the stairs, out, looked back
      at the grand tower, gave a growl,
      and in a spirit of something or other
      sprayed a wall with DONT FORGET.[8]

The most appropriate use made of Spence's towers was in a televised version of Alan Bennett's play *An Englishman Abroad*, about the actor Coral Browne's encounter with the defected traitor Guy Burgess while she was in Moscow in 1958, touring with the Old Vic production of *Hamlet*. Burgess, played by Alan Bates in the play, asks Browne if she would arrange to have a Savile Row suit sent back to him from London when she got home. When the location researcher was looking for a place that would replicate the brutal architecture of the Moscow block in which Burgess was living, they struck gold with one of Basil Spence's Gorbals monsters. The last shot in the play is of Alan Bates in his new glad rags striding along the external concrete corridor of the Queen Elizabeth tower, trying to kid himself that his treason had been worthwhile. I am sure that the betrayal of Gorbals was not part of Alan Bennett's intentions for his play, but it certainly occurred to me as I watched it. The Bennett play was televised in 1983. Ten years later the Spence towers were demolished. They've finally given up on the tower blocks and have reverted to a contemporary version of the tenement, four-storied modern terraces in an attractive variety of styles. That's what I've come to see. And to revive old memories. DONT FORGET! I head for the Glasgow train.

It has to be admitted that the 1960s was an ugly decade for architecture everywhere, not just for the poor. It was characterised by the gestural vanity of many of its practitioners, who seemed to have little reverence for what they had inherited. Queen Street Station in Glasgow was a good example of what they did. Never as handsome as Glasgow's magnificent Central Station, Queen Street had the beauty of its own purpose, till in the 1960s they hid its face behind a hideous mask of concrete that spoiled the grandeur of George Square. When I get off the train, I see it is changed for the better. Now its bold new glass front faces the historic square with confidence and swagger. Not sure I love it. But I like it. Welcome back!

I leave the station, turn into West George Street and head for Buchanan Street. My granny was a Buchanan, but that is not my reason for admiring this street. Over the centuries Glasgow has been knocked about by civic leaders and planners who had little love for the old stones of their town, but the nineteenth and early-twentieth-century city centre is still largely intact, and Buchanan Street is its most prosperous thoroughfare. Uninspiring at its modernised top end, it gets into its stride at St Vincent Street and sweeps you on between lines of confident Victorian buildings. It is still one of Europe's great shopping destinations, but I am not here to shop, so I cross Argyle Street into St Enoch Square. And I am halted by the presence of an absence. This area was once presided over by a railway hotel that made St Pancras in London look timid in comparison. On the east side of the square a curved drive swaggered up to St Enoch's station and the great mansion that fronted it. Opened in 1876, it was closed ninety years later in 1966, a victim of the railway surgery that was the fashion at the time and poured more traffic onto our roads. The hotel and the station, with its twelve platforms and high and sweeping train sheds, were demolished in 1977. Their remains were used as landfill,

and now lie buried beneath the armadillo that is the Scottish Exhibition and Conference Centre at Finnieston Quay, further down the Clyde. In their place was erected a gigantic glass-fronted shopping centre. The only reminder of that era is the red sandstone ticket hall of the old St Enoch subway station, now a Caffè Nero.

DONT FORGET!

I salute the memory and hurry down Dixon Street to the Clyde, aiming for the suspension bridge that will take me to Gorbals. Halfway across I notice two bouquets of faded flowers shoved into the latticed metalwork. Some poor soul must have gone into the water here. Over the years this river has swallowed a lot of Glasgow's pain and sorrow.

> . . . the real Clyde, with a dishrag dawn
> it rinses the horrors of the night
> but cannot make them clean,
> though washing blows
>   where the women watch
> by day,
>   and children run,
>   on Glasgow Green.[9]

At the end of the eighteenth century the Laurie brothers, a couple of enterprising builders, saw an opportunity in attracting the middle classes of Glasgow to a new suburb on the south side of the river, a convenient walk from the city centre. The aristocratic names of the streets they built testify to their ambition, as well their support of

the Union of 1707, probably because it had been good
for business. Some of the street names survive: Eglinton,
Bedford, Norfolk, Cumberland, Oxford. Though the
vision of the Laurie brothers was never fully realised, the
area remained a prosperous middle-class district till well
into the nineteenth century. Abbotsford Place, where I
lived for seven years, was built in 1830, a four-storied
terrace of large apartments, with a mews for horse
carriages round the back. Even as a slum it had a sad
grandeur. All gone, as are the blocks Billy Connolly
described as 'deserts wi windaes', but I am delighted to
discover that they've reinvented the tenement in a bold
new style after those fifty years of arrogant misadventure.

I wander along the new streets, lost, looking for remembered landmarks, wondering where my old church was,
St Margaret's and St Mungo's — Maggie Mungo's to us.

There's no sign of it, but I can see where it was, at the end of a new terrace, next to the Old Woollen Mill in Rutherglen Road. The Mill is now the City Housing Neighbourhood Office. And I am delighted by a piece of street art that recovers the past. I remember a famous photograph taken in 1963 by Oscar Marzaroli, of three Gorbals boys playing in the street, wearing their mothers' high-heel shoes.

It was taken outside a shop in Kidston Street, and it has been recreated by the artist Liz Peden on the corner of Queen Elizabeth Gardens and Cumberland Street: the boys in bronze, their high heels in chrome, in the exact form of the iconic photograph.

There's another piece of public art not far from where Joe, Nicky and Lee played in high heels that day back in 1963. At the entrance of a bold new housing development a bronze four-metre figure of a woman hangs suspended from a roof twenty metres high, stretching between two four-storey modern tenements. She hangs in front of a photograph of a woman walking through a factory towards the camera and above a crypt filled with ashes. Among the ashes are relics of Old Gorbals, including items from the Basil Spence towers. This piece of art is called the Gatekeeper, and it is the work of two artists, Matt Baker and Dan Dubowitz. It gathers the story of Old Gorbals into a concentrated new meaning. I stay beside it for some time, remembering.

DONT FORGET!

I've remembered my yesterdays here fifty years ago, and I am cheered by what I have found today, but before I head back to the train there's another memory I want to recover. Behind where I lived in Abbotsford Place there were two great picture houses across the street from each other, the Coliseum and the New Bedford. What's happened to them?

The back windows of my flat in Abbotsford Place looked out on the New Bedford. It had been built in 1932, at the high point of movie-going in Glasgow. What happened to it? The street system confuses me, but I find my way. I see that the New Bedford is still standing, but it is no longer a picture house. It has been restored and advertises itself as the o2 Academy. Not sure what that means, but it looks good.

But what happened to the Coliseum? It had opened in 1905 as a music hall for Moss's Empire, designed by the theatre architect Frank Matcham. It started showing films in 1925 and was the venue for Glasgow's first talkie in 1929, but it was not fully adapted as a cinema till 1931 for ABC, when they made the auditorium big enough to seat over three thousand, necessary in a city that was the movie-going capital of Britain. In spite of its enormous interior it always felt intimate to me, and its two balconies made it easy to take noisy children to shows without disturbing people in the expensive seats lower down. In 1963 it was chosen as Scotland's first Cinerama theatre, and I was there for the first Cinerama

movie. The film chosen was Stanley Kramer's *It's a Mad, Mad, Mad, Mad World*, and I took a bunch of unruly kids to the Saturday afternoon show. Three hours of slapstick, featuring Spencer Tracy and every famous comedian of the time: Jimmy Durante, Milton Berle, Sid Caesar, Ethel Merman, Buddy Hackett, Mickey Rooney, Jerry Lewis, Phil Silvers, Terry Thomas and many others. We sat in the top balcony and killed ourselves laughing through the whole show.

All gone. I stand in the wasted place where it once stood and ask a passing woman what happened to it. 'It wis wan a' thae listed bildins', she says, 'and they wurrnae allowed tae dae anything wae it', she goes on, 'so it burrnt doon'. Interesting logic. I stand and remember what going to the pictures meant for me.

It was from the back street to the open range,
    from closeness into danger.
It was out of me and into him,
    the solitary boy into the tall rider.

It was a drug, escape,
    hours of dreaming in the mind.
News of 'Future Presentations'
    coming soon – but what was mine?

Then it was down the big, broad stairway,
    At 'The End' into the rain . . .
Now to the palace of my dreaming
    I come back – but it is gone.

Unlike St Kentigern's, there's nothing left to look at and mourn here – only a memory. Strange that I lament the destruction of picture houses as much as the destruction of churches. DONT FORGET! I head for the train.

V

REGRETTING

Though I admire them both, I disagree with Friedrich
Nietzsche and Édith Piaf about regret. Piaf, because
she famously announced in a song that she regretted
nothing – and I don't believe her; Nietzsche, because he
claimed that his:

> . . . formula for greatness in a human being is *amor fati:*
> that one wants nothing to be other than it is, not in the
> future, not in the past, not in all eternity. Not merely
> to endure that which happens of necessity, still less to
> dissemble it . . . but to *love it.*[1]

– and I don't believe him either. No man who could throw
his arms, weeping, round the neck of an old horse being
beaten by its furious owner in a square in Turin, as
Nietzsche did, was practising *amor fati* or love of fate.
Facing reality without flinching, taking what comes upon
oneself with courage, is one thing; claiming that you would
not have it any other way or that it would be wrong even
to *want* it any other way is absurd. Nietzsche was a profound
psychologist of religion and one of its most discerning
critics, but there is something intrinsically religious in the

idea of *amor fati* that brings it close to the different versions of Predestinationism found in both Islam and in some Calvinist versions of Christianity.

Predestinationism is the belief that everything that happens to us has been pre-ordained by the will of God and therefore it must be submitted to. There was probably survival value in believing the doctrine at the time, which might have been what prompted its emergence. In cultures that afforded little opportunity for choice or alteration in one's station in life, the belief that everything had been preordained by God would encourage an attitude of fateful resignation to events, which is probably what its originators intended. Endurance value it may have had, but only by inducing a passive attitude to events, which is why, to recall Edna St Vincent Millay's attitude to death, we should resist it. Even if we acknowledge that the universe and its ultimate weapon, death, gets us all in the end, we should withstand its force as long as we can.

> I am not resigned to the shutting away of loving
>   hearts in the hard ground.
> So it is, and so it will be, for so it has been, time out
>   of mind:
> Into the darkness they go, the wise and the lovely.
>   Crowned
> With lilies and with laurel they go; but I am not
>   resigned.

But was Nietzsche actually preaching resignation, the passive acceptance of everything that comes at us, without challenge? Is that really what *amor fati* is? One of his most recent interpreters does not think so. In her life of Nietzsche, *I Am Dynamite!*, published in 2018, Sue Prideaux explains it this way:

> To love your fate, to accept it and embrace it, was to love and embrace the doctrine of eternal recurrence. This was not, he impishly insisted, to embrace a super- stitious, astrological passivity or a recumbent oriental fatalism, but if man had come to know himself and become himself, then fate must be embraced. If one had character, one had typical experience which also recurred. If life was a long line stretching from the past to the future and one was at a point on this line, one was there through one's own responsibility. This made the conscious soul bound to say yes to this moment and be prepared to be happy that, in the wheel of time, it might recur again and again.[2]

I think I see what she's getting at here. Where we are on that long line stretching from the past to the future is our own responsibility. Our own actions brought us there. Yes, but we were never entirely responsible for the actions that brought us there, any more than we were responsible for our own existence or the circumstances into which we were impelled at birth. That is the secular truth in the idea of Predestinationism. Much if not most of what we became was predetermined by inherited factors and local and historical conditions that were never in our control. True, but if this was the clay we were given to be, with no choice in the matter, we could at least determine some- thing of the shape into which we moulded it. That is what we have to say yes to and even try to love: the given, repetitive self. That is *amor fati*. But if we are to say yes to these recurring moments, these repeated experiences of the self on the wheel of time, it must also mean saying yes to the emotions they provoke, including guilt, sorrow and pity. Yes, and *regret*, regret at the way the wheel pushes the past disappearingly behind us, and regret at all our failures. And, to come back to Nietzsche, it means saying yes to that moment on 3 January 1889, when he left his apartment in Turin and saw a carriage driver beating his horse on the Piazza Carlo Alberto, and threw himself, weeping, around the horse's neck to protect it, the beginning of a descent into a decade of madness he never recovered from. That day in Turin Nietzsche discovered in himself a capacity for overwhelming pity that proved he was not resigned to the sorrows of the world either and refused to say yes to them.

Only psychopaths can live without regret, and we should pity as well as fear them for the lack. Speaking personally, I love the very sound of the word. Like a good poem, it is its own meaning. Just say it, softly: REGRET. Assume all the paradoxes of its meaning: a pleasing sorrow; a loving sadness; an overwhelming yet enriching sense of loss. The capacity for the emotional complexity of regret is one of the most common attributes of melancholia, and it is the dominant mood in poetry, the greatest of the reflective arts. The blind poet Jorge Luis Borges caught the tone perfectly in his poem, 'Possession of Yesterday'.

> I know the things I've lost are so many that I could
>   not begin to count them
>   and that those losses
>   now, are all I have.
> I know that I've lost the yellow and the black and I
>   think
>   of those unreachable colours
>   as those that are not blind can not.
> My father is dead, and always stands beside me.
> When I try to scan Swinburne's verses, I am told, I
>   speak with my
>   father's voice.
> Only those who have died are ours, only what we
>   have lost is ours.
> Ilium vanished, yet Ilium lives in Homer's verses.
> Israel was Israel when it became an ancient
>   nostalgia.
> Every poem, in time, becomes an elegy.

'The women who have left us are ours, free as we
  now are from
misgivings,
    from anguish, from the disquiet and dread of
  hope.
There are no paradises other than lost paradises.[3]

'Every poem, in time, becomes an elegy', and this elegiac
tradition is very strong in English poetry.

With rue my heart is laden
For golden friends I had,
For many a rose-lipt maiden
And many a lightfoot lad.

By brooks too broad for leaping
The lightfoot boys are laid;
The rose-lipt girls are sleeping
In fields where roses fade.[4]

That comes from A.E. Housman, a poet who is the melancholic's melancholic. Alfred Edward Housman was born
in 1859. One of the most distinguished classical scholars
of his day, in 1911 he became Kennedy Professor of Latin
at Trinity College, Cambridge, where he remained for the
rest of his life. A deeply closeted gay man – a necessary
deceit in those punitive, intolerant times – he was the
author of many poems plangent with loss and regret, and
subtly tinged with anger. Why the anger? Because he hated
the cold, indifferent destructiveness of death and longed
for the Christian hope of eternal life to be true – but knew

it wasn't. It was said of him that he was an atheist who looked hungrily at the Christian world, but refused to swallow its food.' But: 'If atheism takes away immortal hope, it gives other things: the eye looks with a keener glance at transitory beauty: it sees more sharply the splendour as well as the pathos of human effort; it loves things more because they die.'[6] In other words, it knows regret, and even claims to speak it on behalf of the dead, who, by dying, have lost everything.

> The farms of home lie lost in even,
> I see far off the steeple stand;
> West and away from here to heaven
> Still is the land.

> There if I go no girl will greet me,
> No comrade hollo from the hill,
> No dog run down the yard to meet me:
> The land is still.

> The land is still by farm and steeple,
> And still for me the land may stay:
> There I was friends with perished people,
> And there lie they.[7]

Yes, death takes us away to lie and moulder in the earth, but till it comes for us there are fleeting joys to experience.

> Loveliest of trees, the cherry now
> Is hung with bloom along the bough,

And stands about the woodland ride
Wearing white for Eastertide.

Now, of my threescore years and ten,
Twenty will not come again,
And take from seventy springs a score,
It only leaves me fifty more.

And since to look at things in bloom
Fifty years are little room,
About the woodland I will go
To see the cherry hung with snow.[8]

Among English poets, the other great charismatic melancholic and laureate of regret was John Betjeman, whom we met mourning in Cornwall in the second chapter. Betjeman's poetic depth and subtlety were often overlooked because his poems were so popular. His biographer, A.N. Wilson, discusses one of his great yet underrated poems.

Three years after Betjeman married, King George V died, and it inspired one of the best public poems of the twentieth century. Who can doubt that, in the final stanza, Betjeman is thinking of those ramrod-straight, decent figures who shored up the British Empire in its last phases? In twelve lines, he captures the dullness of the late king – his shooting, his stamps, his obsession with correct dress; and the momentous nature of the change, the final putting to sleep of the Victorian age as, at Croydon airport, the anarchic and 'unsuitable' figure of Edward VIII, with his flash clothes, divorced mistress and alleged fascistic leanings, arrives. None of these things is spelt out, they are all implied in the essential simplicity of the lyric form.[9]

The title of the poem he is describing is: 'Death of King George V – "New King arrives in his capital by air . . ." *Daily Newspaper*'.

> Spirits of well-shot woodcock, partridge, snipe
>   Flutter and bear him up the Norfolk sky:
> In that red house in a red mahogany bookcase
>   The stamp collection waits with mounts long dry.
>
> The big blue eyes are shut which saw wrong clothing
>   And favourite fields and coverts from a horse;
> Old men in country houses hear clocks ticking
>   Over thick carpets with a deadened force.
>
> Old men who never cheated, never doubted,
>   Communicated monthly, sit and stare
> At the new suburb stretched beyond the run-way
>   Where a young man lands hatless from the air.[10]

I probably ought to mention that 'Communicated monthly' does not refer to the occasional phone call or scribbled letter, but to the old low-church Anglican habit of receiving Holy Communion once a month, according to the rites of the 1662 version of *The Book of Common Prayer*.

The poetry of regret can be as varied and particular as human experience itself, but it comes in two dominant forms. As with this Betjeman poem, there is regret at the passing of time and what it takes from us through death, as well as through those inexorable shifts in culture and technology that can change the style of a once-loved and remembered street. Then there is personal regret at the losses of broken relationships and personal failure. Irish poets are the supreme laureates of both modes of regret, and one of the greatest was Louis MacNeice, born in Belfast in 1907. He gives us the early part of his own biography in the poem 'Carrickfergus':

I was born in Belfast between the mountain and the
    gantries
        To the hooting of lost sirens and the clang of
    trams:
Thence to Smoky Carrick in County Antrim
        Where the bottle-neck harbour collects the mud
    which jams

The little boats beneath the Norman castle,
        The pier shining with lumps of crystal salt;
The Scotch Quarter was a line of residential houses
        But the Irish Quarter was a slum for the blind
    and halt.

The brook ran yellow from the factory stinking of
    chlorine,
        The yarn-mill called its funeral cry at noon;
Our lights looked over the lough to the lights of
    Bangor
        Under the peacock aura of a drowning moon.

The Norman walled the town against the country
    To stop his ears to the yelping of his slave
And built a church in the form of a cross but
    denoting
        The list of Christ on the cross in the angle of
        the nave.

I was the rector's son, born to the Anglican order,
    Banned for ever from the candles of the Irish
    poor;
The Chichesters knelt in marble at the end of the
    transept
        With ruffs about their necks, their portion sure.

The war came and a huge camp of soldiers
    Grew from the ground in sight of our house
    with long
Dummies hanging from gibbets for bayonet
    practice
        And the sentry's challenge echoing all day long;

A Yorkshire terrier ran in and out by the gate-lodge
    Barred to civilians, yapping as if taking affront:
Marching at ease and singing 'Who Killed Cock
    Robin?'
        The troops went out by the lodge and off to the
        Front.

The steamer was camouflaged that took me to
    England –
        Sweat and khaki in the Carlisle train;

I thought that the war would last for ever and sugar
    Be always rationed and that never again

Would the weekly papers not have photos of sand-
    bags
    And my governess not make bandages from moss
And people not have maps above the fireplace
    With flags on pins moving across and across –

Across the hawthorn hedge the noise of bugles,
    Flares across the night,
Somewhere on the lough was a prison ship for
    Germans,
    A cage across their sight.

I went to school in Dorset, the world of parents
    Contracted into a puppet world of sons
Far from the mill girls, the smell of porter, the salt-
    mines
    And the soldiers with their guns.[11]

What he does not mention in that poem, as the defining moment of his life at the age of five, was the sudden disappearance of his mother and her subsequent death in hospital, both without explanation to the grieving child.

In my childhood trees were green
And there was plenty to be seen.

Come back early or never come.

My father made the walls resound,
He wore his collar the wrong way round.

Come back early or never come.

My mother wore a yellow dress;
Gentle, gently, gentleness.

Come back early or never come.

When I was five the black dreams came;
Nothing after was quite the same.

Come back early or never come.

The dark was talking to the dead;
The lamp was dark beside my bed.

Come back early or never come.

When I woke they did not care;
Nobody, nobody was there.

Come back early or never come.

When my silent terror cried,
Nobody, nobody replied.

Come back early or never come.

I got up; the chilly sun

Saw me walk away alone.

Come back early or never come.[12]

The first MacNeice poem I fell in love with was 'Snow'. Apart from the beauty and surprise of it, it appealed to me philosophically. I did not know at the time that it also represented the intellectual complexity of its author's thinking and attitude to life. Or, and this is a better way of putting it, that it represented his grasp of the complexity of reality and how we should be open to all its crazy and incorrigible plurality, unlike the tidy universes of history's ideological zealots.

The room was suddenly rich and the great bay-
    window was
Spawning snow and pink roses against it
Soundlessly collateral and incompatible:
World is suddener than we fancy it.

World is crazier and more of it than we think,
Incorrigibly plural. I peel and portion
A tangerine and spit the pips and feel
The drunkenness of things being various.

And the fire flames with a bubbling sound for
    world
Is more spiteful and gay than one supposes –
On the tongue on the eyes on the ears in the palms
    of one's
        hands –

There is more than glass between the snow and the
    huge roses.[13]

MacNeice died too early in 1963, aged fifty-five. His death
prompted an act of devotion from three of his fellow
Irish poets that resulted in the composition of another
stunning elegy. The story is that Seamus Heaney, Michael
Longley and Derek Mahon visited MacNeice's grave in
County Down not long after his death, each one contem-
plating an elegy for their dead friend. Mahon read his first,
echoing lines from MacNeice's 'Snow'. Heaney then began
to read his, but stopped and crumpled it up. Longley
decided not even to attempt his, declaring Mahon's elegy
'definitive'.[14] Here it is.

In Carrowdore Churchyard
(at the grave of Louis MacNeice)

Your ashes will not stir, even on this high ground,
However the wind tugs, the headstones shake.
The plot is consecrated, for your sake,
To what lies in the future tense. You lie
Past tension now, and spring is coming round
Igniting flowers on the peninsula.

Your ashes will not fly, however the winds roar
Through elm and bramble. Soon the biographies
And buried poems will begin to appear,
But we pause here to remember the lost life.
Maguire proposes a blackbird in low relief
Over the grave, and a phrase from Euripides.

Which suits you down to the ground. Like this
  churchyard
With its play of shadow, its humane perspective.
Locked in the winter's fist, these hills are hard
As nails, yet soft and feminine in their turn
When fingers open and the hedges burn.
This, you implied, is how we ought to live –

The ironical, loving crush of roses against snow,
Each fragile, solving ambiguity. So
From the pneumonia of the ditch, from the ague
Of the blind poet and the bombed town you bring
The all-clear to the empty holes of spring,
Rinsing the choked mud, keeping the colours new.[15]

Derek Mahon, who died in 2020 while I was composing
this book, was a master of the poetry of regret in both
its forms: regret at the passing of time and what it takes
away with it, and regret at personal failure and the heart-
break it causes. Here's how he described 'Brian Moore's
Belfast'.

The last trams were still running in those days.
People wore hats and gloves as long before;
raw fissures lingered where incendiaries
demolished Clifton St in April of '41:
the big band era, dances and commotion,
but the war ended and rain swept once more
parks and playgrounds, chapel and horse trough
'to die in faraway mists over Belfast Lough'.

Do this, do that, road closed, no entry, stop! –
a world of signs and yet the real thing too:
even now I catch a whiff of brack and bap,
the soap and ciggies of the *disparus.*
Buns from Stewart's, gobstoppers from Graham's,
our crowd intent on our traditional games,
sectarian puzzlement, a swinging rope,
freezing winters, pristine bicycle frames;

school windows under the Cave Hill, childish faces,
uncles and aunties, pipes and lipstick traces,
epiphanies in sheds and woody places:
how can we not love the first life we knew?
'We can dream only what we know', he said.
I know the whole length of the Antrim Road
and often think of Salisbury Avenue;
mysterious Hazelwood, I still dream of you.

On Riverside Drive and a California dream beach
such things revisited him, just out of reach,
just as he left them after Naples, Warsaw,
frozen for ever in the austere post-war
where frequent silence keeps its own integrity
and smoky ghosts of the exhausted city
rustle with phantom life whose time is up.
They queue in Campbell's crowded coffee shop

or wait for a bus at Robb's. I can make out
a clutch of gantries, a white sepulchre
grimly vigilant on its tiny acre,
skirts and shirts mid-20th-century style

in dimly lit arcades, carpets of wet
grain at the quayside where a night boat
churns up the dark and a rapturous old girl
sings 'Now is the Hour' with her eternal smile.[16]

But for me Mahon's most perfect and devastating poem
is a supreme example of the regret for personal failure
and loss. It is a letter to his children Rory and Katie.
Compose yourself before reading it. Touch your own
regrets. It's called 'Yaddo, or A Month in the Country'.

We are born in an open field and we die in a dark wood.
    Russian proverb.

Here among the lakes and dripping pines
off Route 9P, I write you guys these lines
to ask you what you're up to and what not.
No doubt I'll finish them in my attic flat

in Dublin, if I ever get back there
to the damp gardens of Fitzwilliam Square.
Do you still like your London schools? Do you
still slam the goals in, Rory? Katie-coo,
how goes it with the piano and flute?
I've a composer in the next-door suite
composing string quartets, an English novelist,
a sculptor from Vermont and a young ceramist
from Kansas; for we come in suns and snows
from *everywhere* to write, paint and compose.
Sport? We've a pool, closed till the end of May,
a tennis court where no one seems to play;
though there's a horse show, among other things,
starting next week in Saratoga Springs
just down the road – a fascinating place
with spas and concerts and a certain grace.
Also a certain measure of renown
since it was here, in an open field north of the town,
that Philip Schuyler clobbered John Burgoyne
in 1777, two hundred and thirteen years ago,
thus helping to precipitate the America we know.
But you're not interested in that kind of stuff;
like me, you'd rather go to the movies for a laugh –
or would you? We talk so infrequently
I hardly know where your real interests lie.
What, for example, are you reading now?
John Buchan? Molly Keane? *Catch-22*?
Nothing too highbrow, time enough for that:
you're better off with a flute or a cricket bat.
You're only (only!) in your middle teens,
too young to be thinking about *seerious* things

like the dream plays and ghost sonatas your
lost father hears and watches everywhere,
especially when he glimpses happy families
a-picnicking among the squirrel trees.
I try to imagine you asleep, at work,
or walking with your mother in Hyde Park
where once we walked each Sunday, hand in hand,
to feed the daffy ducks on the Round Pond,
chucking crumbs to the ones we liked the best,
comical, tufted yellow-eyes, ignoring all the rest.
Remember birthday parties, rockets at Hallowe'en,
bus-rides to Covent Garden to see Eugene?
The day we drove to Brighton? Maybe not.
Summer and winter I would rise and trot
my fingers up your back like a mad mouse
to wake you chuckling. Now I wake in a silent house
in a dark wood. Once, 'Is it morning time?'
asked Katie waking. Now it is mourning time
in a black heart; but I will not forget
the nooks and corners of our crazy flat,
its dormer windows and its winding stair,
gulls on the roof, its view of *everywhere!*
When mummy and I split up and I lived in Co. Cork
among the yacht crowd and bohemian folk
I'd wander round the hills above Kinsale
where English forces clobbered Hugh O'Neill
or dander down along the Bandon River
wondering when next we'd be together;
then home to a stable loft where I could hear
mysterious night sounds whispering in my ear –
woodpigeons, foxes, silence, my own brain,

my lamp a lighthouse in the drizzling rain.
After a month of fog a day would dawn
when the rain ceased, cloud cleared and the sun
    shone;
then magical white wisps of smoke would rise
and I'd think of our magical London years.
'One always loses with a desperate throw':
what I lost was a wife, a life, and you.
As for love, a treasure when first it's new,
it all too often fades away, for both, like the morning
    dew;
yet it remains the one sure thing to cling to
as I cling for dear life to the thought of you,
sitting alone here in upstate New York
halfway to Montreal, trying to work,
lit by Tiffany lamps, Sinéad O'Connor on the
    stereo.
This above all, to thine own selves be true,
remembering seaside games in stormy Ulster parts
with lemonade for you in paper cups,
snooker and candlelight for the 'grown-ups'.
Your father (yawn!) has seen enough mischance
trying to figure out the dancers from the dance.
Like Mummy, *some* can dance; I never could,
no more than I could ever see the birches for the
    wood.
We are *all* children; and when either of you
feels scared or miserable, as you must sometimes do,
look to us, but remember we do too.
I hear the big trucks flashing through the night
like Christmas road-houses ablaze with light,

symbols of modern movement and romance;
but the important thing is permanence –
for you, a continuity with the past
enabling you to prosper, and a fast
forward to where the paradoxes grow
like crocuses in our residual snow;
for me, a long devotion to the art
in which you play such an important part,
a long devotion to the difficult Muse
your mother was, despite our difficulties.
Everything thrives in contrariety – no
thesis without antithesis; no black
without its white, like a hot sun on the ice in Yaddo
   lake.
Children of light, may your researches be
reflections on this old anomaly;
may you remember, as the years go by
and you go slowly towards maturity,
that life consists in the receipt of life,
its fun and games, its boredom and its grief;
that no one, sons or daughters, fathers, wives,
escapes the rough stuff that makes up our lives.
Equip yourselves in every way you can
to take it like a woman or a man,
respecting values you've long understood
pertaining to the true, the beautiful and the good.
Sorry to sound so tedious and trite.
I'd hoped to be more fun and try to write
you something entertaining as I often try to do;
but this time round I wanted to be *seerious* and true
to felt experience. My love 2U.

Nothing I say you don't already know.
Football and flute, you'll join us soon enough
in the mad 'grown-up' world of Henry James' 'stupid
    life'.
Write soon and tell me all about your work.
It's time now for your father to be heading for New
    York,
a city worse than London, rife with confrontation,
much like the one you see on television.
Maybe I'll read this letter at the 'Y'
and tell you all about it by and by.
I hope I haven't bored you stiff already.
Write to me soon in Dublin.

           My love, as ever,
              – Daddy.[17]

One way to account for the power and reach of these great Irish elegists is to remember what Auden said of Yeats, that it was mad Ireland that hurt him into poetry. Well, Ireland has no monopoly on the pain that transmutes itself into great art. Life can perform that miracle anywhere. I'll leave it to MacNeice to say why.

I am not yet born: O hear me.
Let not the bloodsucking bat or the rat or the stoat
    or the
        club-footed ghoul come near me.

I am not yet born, console me.
I fear that the human race may with tall walls wall
    me,

with strong drugs dope me, with wise lies lure
me,
on black racks rack me, in blood-baths roll me.

I am not yet born; provide me
With water to dandle me, grass to grow for me, trees
to talk
to me, sky to sing to me, birds and a white
light
in the back of my mind to guide me.

I am not yet born; forgive me
For the sins that in me the world shall commit, my
words
when they speak me, my thoughts when they
think me,
my treason engendered by traitors beyond
me,
my life when they murder by means of my
hands, my death when they live me.

I am not yet born; rehearse me
In the parts I must play and the cues I must take
when
old men lecture me, bureaucrats hector me,
mountains
frown at me, lovers laugh at me, the white
waves call me to folly and the desert calls
me to doom and the beggar refuses
my gift and my children curse me.

I am not yet born; O hear me,
Let not the man who is beast or who thinks he is
  God
    come near me.

I am not yet born; O fill me
With strength against those who would freeze my
    humanity, would dragoon me into a legal
  automaton,
      would make me a cog in a machine, a thing with
      one face, a thing, and against all those
      who would dissipate my entirety, would
      blow me like thistledown hither and
      thither or hither and thither
      like water held in the
      hands would spill me.

Let them not make me a stone and let them not spill
    me.
Otherwise kill me.[18]

'I am not yet born; forgive me
For the sins that in me the world shall commit . . .'

If we need forgiveness before we are born it is because
we do not know who we are until we discover that we
need it – and know ourselves for the first time. In the
world's literature of regret, a poignant example was Peter
the Apostle, the man who did not know he was a betrayer
– till he betrayed.

We don't know who we are
till the first betrayal and the second,
and the third – at the cock's crow.
Then we know.

VI

FORGIVING

Being human is complicated. However we account for its emergence, nature has endowed humans with a high intelligence and the self-consciousness that goes with it. And it has made us an object of interest to ourselves in a way that does not seem to be the case with the other animals on the planet. Let me count a few of the ways in which this characteristic reveals itself.

With some endearing and eccentric exceptions, most humans are concerned about their appearance, with how they look, and whole industries have developed round that concern. The fashion industry is an obvious example, but a more fascinating and topical example is the beauty industry. Until recently it confined itself to what were essentially disguises or cover ups, such as cosmetics and hair styling. Now surgical interventions are available that can permanently alter a person's appearance or remove some of the physical effects of ageing – often with tragic results. One of the most depressing experiences of contemporary culture is to catch a glimpse on television of a former Hollywood star whose ageing face has been ravaged by bouts of plastic surgery, testimony to the human obsession with appearance and the lengths to which we'll go to improve it. The other animals we share the planet with have been spared the narcissistic sorrows of this kind of self-awareness. D.H. Lawrence caught the difference in four spare lines.

> I never saw a wild thing
> sorry for itself.
> A small bird will drop frozen dead from a bough
> without ever having felt sorry for itself.[1]

At a deeper and more estimable level, we are also obsessed with how we ought to live, and how we should understand ourselves and the universe in which we find ourselves, a universe that does not talk about itself – except through us. As far as we can tell from our own investigations, it is only in us that the universe has started thinking or wondering about itself. This points to the inevitable circularity that characterises our investigations into the nature of the reality we inhabit. Whatever we discover about the world is mediated through our minds, and often it is hard to separate what is discovered from the minds that do the discovering, a conundrum that is particularly strong in the struggles of the moral life.

What is required of us, we wonder? And what is the nature of the force that does the requiring? Does it have objective reality and authority over us, or has it been generated by the convolutions of our own minds? How can we trust its authority if, as seems likely, we ourselves have invented or imagined its existence in order to satisfy our own needs or appease our own fears? This is the anxiety that accompanies human self-consciousness. And it is why we are such a disputatious and unhappy species. We never seem able to get out of our own way. The other animals don't suffer from this angst. They live with an unself-conscious immediacy that enables them to stay tuned to nature and its demands without guilt or hesitation. It was recognising this that transported the American poet Mark Doty from a Massachusetts shopping mall to – well, where exactly?

Near evening, in Fairhaven, Massachusetts,
seventeen wild geese arrowed the ashen blue
over the Walmart and the Blockbuster Video,

and I was up there, somewhere between the asphalt
and their clear dominion – not in the parking lot,
its tallowy circles just appearing,

the shopping carts shining, from above,
like little scraps of foil. Their eyes
held me there, the unfailing gaze

of those who know how to fly in formation,
wing-tip to wing-tip, safe, fearless.
And the convex glamour of their eyes carried

the parking lot, the wet field
troubled with muffler shops
and stoplights, the arc of highway

and its exits, one shattered farmhouse

with its failing barn . . . The wind
a few hundred feet above the grass

erases the mechanical noises, everything;
nothing but their breathing
and the perfect rowing of the pinions,

and then, out of that long, percussive pour
toward what they are most certain of,
comes their – question, is it?

Assertion, prayer, aria – as delivered
by something too compelled in its passage
to sing? A hoarse and unwieldy music

that plays nonetheless down the length
of me until I am involved in their flight,
the unyielding necessity of it, as they literally

rise above, ineluctable, heedless,
needing nothing . . . Only animals
make me believe in God now

– so little between spirit and skin,
any gesture so entirely themselves.
But I wasn't with them,

as they headed toward Acushnet
and New Bedford, of course I wasn't,
though I was not exactly in the parking lot

either, where the cars nudged in and out
of their slots, each taking the place another
had abandoned, so that no space, no desire

would remain unfulfilled. I wasn't there.
I was so filled with longing
– is that what that sound is for?

I seemed to be nowhere at all.[2]

Humans are rarely capable of living in that state of unself-
conscious, ecstatic immediacy. Our restless intelligence
conjures up worlds of conflict and confusion for us, as
we dispute the very ideas we ourselves devise to explain
ourselves to ourselves. One of the most penetrating
descriptions of the complexity of the human condition
came from an Elizabethan nobleman, Fulke Greville, Lord
Brooke (1554–1628).

Oh wearisome condition of Humanity!
Born under one law, to another bound;

Vainly begot, and yet forbidden vanity;
Created sick, commanded to be sound:
What meaneth Nature by these diverse laws?
Passion and Reason self-division cause:
Is it the mark or majesty of Power
To make offences that it may forgive?
Nature herself doth her own self deflower,
To hate those errors she herself doth give.
For how should man think that he may not do,
If Nature did not fail, and punish too?
Tyrant to others, to herself unjust,
Only commands things difficult and hard,
Forbids us all things which it knows is lust,
Makes easy pains, impossible reward.
If Nature did not take delight in blood,
She would have made more easy ways to good.
We that are bound by vows and by promotion,
With pomp of holy sacrifice and rites,
To teach belief in good and still devotion,
To preach of Heaven's wonders and delights:
Yet when each of us in his own heart looks,
He finds the God there, far unlike his books.[5]

In this poem, Fulke Greville reflects rather than resolves
the frustrations and contradictions in human experience.
Predetermined by natural forces and social circumstances
that were never under our control, certain versions of
religion have taught us to feel guilty for the results.

Nature herself doth her own self deflower,
To hate those errors she herself doth give.

For how should man think that he may not do,
If Nature did not fail, and punish too?
Tyrant to others, to herself unjust,
Only commands things difficult and hard,
Forbids us all things which it knows is lust,
Makes easy pains, impossible reward.

Here he was almost certainly referring to a Christian interpretation of the ancient parable of Adam and Eve, who
ate the fruit of the forbidden tree, became sexual creatures
as a consequence, and thereby incurred a guilt they trans-
mitted to all who came after them. Guilty of what? *Of
having been being born.* But why was being born a sin? Because
generation is a sexual act energised by lust, and lust was
the original sin or the sin that *originated* us, and it can only
be redeemed by a supernatural intervention. Let me spin
the syllogism thus:

The procreative act is a sin that transmits guilt to all
    who are born.
I have been born.
Therefore, I am guilty.

It does not matter that this syllogistic monstrosity is based
on a literalist reading of the myth of the Garden of Eden
in the Book of Genesis; it is the consequence in human
history that matters; and the consequence was that in
significant elements of the Christian tradition a special
suspicion attached itself to the reproductive urge and
through it to the human being or to being human. Having
been born rendered us guilty of a primordial crime whose

punishment would be damnation, unless we enrolled ourselves in the divine salvation system. A central part of the system involved the complete abnegation of sex by the holy, alongside a concessionary system that permitted its performance for purposes of procreation by 'those who did not possess the gift of continence'. A prohibition, as all prohibitions do, that increased the fascination of the forbidden act, and sent it into the shadows.

It does not take much insight to acknowledge that, given the self-involved nature of their consciousness, humans easily get their instinctive drives out of balance with nature. Let me count the ways. Our capacity for apocalyptic violence is the supreme example of this tragic distortion, turning the instinct for self-defence into geno-cidal destructions that have wrecked civilisations and uprooted millions of people down the ages. That's not all. We need to eat in order to live, but that can easily get twisted into living in order to eat, or eating compulsively to satisfy other less easily identifiable needs. At the oppo-site end of the spectrum of eating disorders is the paradox of the enduring co-existence of the overfed and the starving in the same world, a dissonance as ancient as scripture.

Sex is the third element in this trio of instincts that can go so easily astray in humans. The difference is that sex is the only one of the three that we have been persuaded to see as intrinsically wrong; or, to be closer to the truth, the only one of the three that *certain versions of religion* have seen as intrinsically evil, as sinful in itself. At its rawest, the teaching was that a baby, simply by virtue of having been born, was the object of God's wrath. Fortunately,

Christianity's instinct for kindness usually moderates its instinct for harshness, and that was the case here. You experience the muddle at its best in Christmas carols, where the prevailing tone is one of joyous rescue from an evil fate through the loving intervention of God. The fact that it was God who conceived the evil fate he is now rescuing us from is never spelled out in geometric detail, almost as if there was a determined effort not to spoil the fun; but you can see it in the beautiful puzzles the carols create for themselves. You find it in the elisions of this traditional English carol.

This is the truth sent from above
The truth of God, the God of love;
Therefore don't turn me from your door,
But hearken all, both rich and poor.

The first thing which I do relate,
Is that God did man create;
The next thing, which to you I'll tell,
Woman was made with man to dwell.

Then after that 'twas God's own choice
to place them both in paradise,
there to remain from evil free
except they ate from such a tree.

But they did eat, which was a sin,
and thus their ruin did begin –
ruined themselves, both you and me,
and all of our posterity.

Thus we were heirs to endless woes,
Till God the Lord did interpose;
And so a promise soon did run
That he would redeem us by his Son.

And at that season of the year
Our blest Redeemer did appear;
Here he did live, and here did preach,
And many thousands he did teach.

Thus he in love to us behaved,
To show us how we must be saved;
And if you want to know the way
Be pleased to hear what he did say.

'Go preach the gospel,' now he said,
'to all nations that are made!
And those that do believe in me,
from all their sins I'll set them free.'

O seek! O seek of God above
that saving faith that works by love!
And, if he's pleased to grant thee this,
Thou't sure to have eternal bliss.

God grant to all within this place
true saving faith, that special grace
which to his people doth belong:
and thus I close my Christmas song.

We are reading folk poetry here, so we should not be too forensic about the detail, but the obvious conclusion to draw is that the sin of Adam and Eve in the Garden of Eden did not just ruin the original couple, it ruined 'both you and me, and all of our posterity', as the carol puts it. It claims that, by virtue of having been born, we have inherited the guilt of Adam and are on the way to eternal damnation – unless God chooses to redeem us. Recent generations of theologians have been good at demytholo-gising the story in a way that allows us to go on reading it as a parable of the human condition, and no longer as the report of an allegedly deadly historic event.

What they have found it more difficult to do is to remove the stain its original interpretation imprinted on human sexuality, in the Christian tradition, because procreation became inevitably associated with guilt. Another tragic aspect of this way of doing theology is that it gave to human life a purposeful, eschatological turn. Life was no longer something we could enjoy in its immediacy for its own sake, like the other animals on earth. Life was now understood as a selection process in which success would guarantee eternal bliss, failure, eternal woe. It kept everyone enrolled in the course looking ahead, always ahead, to the moment when the results would finally come in.

The philosopher Isaiah Berlin understood what a waste of time this was, a waste of *our* time as it runs away from us or as we run through it. It was the tragedy of all escha-tological thinking, the kind of thinking that removes us from 'now' to 'then', the tragedy being that, since 'then' never arrives, we are wasting all our 'nows' – since *now* is always where we find ourselves. This is how Berlin expressed it in an essay on the Russian thinker, Alexander Herzen.

> Who will find fault with nature because flowers bloom in the morning and die at night, because she has not given the rose or the lily the hardness of flint? . . . If you look beyond your pleasure in it . . . for some other goal, the moment will come when the singer stops and then you will only have memories and vain regrets because, instead of listening, you were waiting for something else . . . We think the purpose of the child is to grow up because it does grow up. But its purpose is to play, to enjoy itself, to be a child. If we merely look at the end of the process, the purpose of all life is death.[4]

What has happened here? We can overplay the point Berlin was making. There is value, and there can even be joy in purposive activity. But his central point is valid. *Life is its own meaning*, so it is a waste to spend it getting ready for another life beyond that almost certainly won't come. Behind the mistake is a failure to understand the difference between humanity's two greatest creations, art and science. Art is the imaginative way we reflect on or represent our complicated nature and play it back to ourselves. We write fictions and make pictures that show us how we are, and we say to ourselves: Aren't they beautiful? Aren't they tragic? Aren't they complex? Ponder them. Learn from them. See how they show us how things are with us.

That is not how science operates. Science is less interested in reflecting the universe back at itself than in trying to figure out how it works. It does not just stand in the parking lot at Walmart's in Fairhaven, Massachusetts, ecstatically transported by the sight of migrating geese; it seeks to understand the nature of migration; what its purpose is; how it works. Scientists may be moved by the sight of migrating geese, but their main passion is wanting to know where they are going, and why.

A good place to start negotiating the difference between the truth of art and the truth of science is with George Orwell's political parable *Animal Farm,* written in 1945. Orwell wrote his book as a critique of the ruthlessness of Stalinist Russia. It tells the story of a group of animals who rebel against the farmer who owns them, in order to create a perfect society where all animals will be equal, free and happy. The revolution does not work out that way, and the farm ends up as unequal as it was before, if not worse, under the dictatorship of a pig called Napoleon. Was *Animal Farm* true, did it actually happen? It depends what you mean by *true.* It didn't happen in *history* as described, but yes, it gave a true account of human nature. It was what scholars call a myth. A myth is not a lie. It is a fiction through which a perennial truth is communicated. It is a made-up story intended to cast an honest light on the human condition.

Tragically, a failure or refusal to understand how myths work crept into Christianity during its early years. Its leaders started claiming that these ancient writings were not *art,* the imaginative expression of enduring truths about the human condition; they were reports of events that had happened precisely as described, right down to a talking snake and a god who walked in a garden in the cool of the early evening. The story of Adam and Eve in the Garden of Eden was converted from a useful fiction about the turbulent discontents that characterise our relationships, into a dangerous assertion of historical fact. Here is the moment in Genesis at the root of the mistake.

> The Lord God called to the man, and said to him, 'Where are you?' He said, 'I heard the sound of you in the garden, *and I was afraid, because I was naked;* and I hid myself.' He said, 'Who told you that you were naked? Have you eaten of the tree of which I commanded you not to eat?' The man said, 'The woman whom thou gavest to be with me, she gave me fruit from the tree, and I ate.'[5]

The gentlest way to read that story is to understand it as a coming-of-age parable, the shift from pre-sexual innocence to the sorrows and raptures of adulthood. So, what happened? Why did we stop reading it as a true fiction and start reading it as a report of an actual event? Nietzsche described how the process started and the loss that resulted.

> . . . it is the lot of all myths to creep gradually into the confines of a supposedly historical reality, and to be treated by some later age as unique fact with claims to historical truth . . . this is how religions tend to die: the mythic premises of a religion are systematized, beneath the stern and intelligent eyes of an orthodox dogmatism, into a fixed sum of historical events; one begins nervously defending the veracity of myths, at the same time resisting their continuing life and growth. The feeling

for myth dies and is replaced by religious claims to foundation in history.[6]

And what a waste of inspiration it was. When dogmatists insist that religion can only be practised as the science of supernatural salvation, they lose the multitudes who might benefit from following it as a heuristic art, an art that gives form to the longings and complexities of human existence, an art that offers the only immortality many of us are interested in. In his play *Travesties,* Tom Stoppard puts this justification of art into the mouth of James Joyce, in a speech about Homer's *Odyssey*:

> An artist is the magician put among men to gratify – capriciously – their urge for immortality. The temples are built and brought down around him, continuously and contiguously, from Troy to the fields of Flanders. If there is any meaning in any of it, it is in what survives as art, yes even in the celebration of tyrants, yes even in the celebration of nonentities . . . What now of the Trojan War if it had been passed over by the artist's touch? Dust . . .[7]

Poets understand this. They know that all our Edens are lost Edens. Here is one of them, thinking himself back into that lost and remembered garden.

> It's hard to remember one was ever there,
> Or what was supposed to be so great about it.
> Each morning a newly minted sun rose
> In a new sky, and birdsong filled the air.

There were all these things to name, and no sex.
The children took what God had given them –
A world held in common, a form of life
Without sin or moral complexity,
A vernal paradise complete with snakes –
And sold it all for a song, for the glory
Of the knowledge contained in the fatal apple.
At any rate, that's the official story.

In Masaccio's fresco in the Brancacci Chapel
The figures are smaller than you'd expect
And lack context, and seem all the more tragic.
The Garden is implicit in their faces,
Depicted through the evasive magic
Of the unpresented. Eve's arm is slack
And hides her sex. There isn't much to see
Beyond that, for the important questions,
The questions to which one constantly comes
   back,
Aren't about their lost, undepicted home,
But the ones framed by their distorted mouths:
What are we now? What will we become?

Think of it as whatever state preceded
The present moment, this prison of the self.
The idea of the Garden is the idea
Of something tangible which has receded
Into stories, into poetry.
As one ages, it becomes less a matter
Of great intervals than of minor moments
Much like today's, which time's strange geometry

Has rendered unreal. And yet the question,
Raised anew each day, is the same one,
Though the person raising it isn't the same:
What am I now? What have I become?[8]

The mythologies created by human art are constantly asking, in Koethe's words: *'What am I now? What have I become?'* But when dogmatic theologians insist on transubstantiating them from useful fictions into absurd assertions of fact, they render them useless to many of us. No wonder Nietzsche despised religion's capacity for inducing such conflict and confusion in the human animal and proposed, instead, his doctrine of *amor fati*. So, let us have another look at it and see where it takes us this time. Here it is again:

. . . my formula for greatness in a human being is *amor fati:* that one wants nothing to be other than it is, not in the future, not in the past, not in all eternity. Not merely to endure that which happens of necessity, still less to dissemble it . . . but to *love it.*[9]

The Nietzschean scholar Walter Kaufmann unpacks the meaning for us:

The projection of one's feeling towards oneself upon a cosmic scale may seem to hinge on a metaphysical premise, but it can be defended empirically. That I am here, now, doing this – that depends on an awe-inspiring series of antecedent events, on millions of seemingly accidental moves and decisions, both by myself and many others whose moves and decisions in turn depended on yet other people. And our very existence, our being as we are, required that our parents had to choose each other, not anyone else, and beget us at the precise moment when we were actually begotten; and the same consideration applies to their parents, and to all our ancestors, going back indefinitely.[10]

None of the facts that went into our origins were under our control; yet, had we been able to run them through some kind of predictive algorithm, we could probably have anticipated what we became and the behaviour that resulted. It is this combination of the unpredictable and the predetermined that writes the story of an actual human life. And if we want to say yes to our own existence, we have to say yes to all of it, including what we look back on with shame. This act of self-understanding leads to self-acceptance, an activity that has been given added impetus by the relatively recent discipline of psychoanalysis, designed to help us answer the questions: how did I get to be like this and is there anything I can do about it? Or, in John Koethe's formulation: *'What am I now? What have I become?'* Historians apply similar techniques to human history, performing a kind of collective psychoanalysis. Autobiographical writers perform the same kind of excavations on themselves. A notable recent example came from Simon Gray, in a series of short books he wrote as he looked back at his life and observed his death from cancer, after a lifetime of heroic smoking. Echoing T.S. Eliot's lines from 'Burnt Norton':

> Time present and time past
> Are both perhaps present in time future,
> And time future contained in time past.[11]

Gray wrote,

> Our beginnings never know our ends, quoting T.S. Eliot . . . and it seems to me that it's probably also true that our ends never know our beginnings – well, how can we? As we never know when our beginnings began. I don't mean just the seminal fuck, which is often the end of something else, a vile row or a stretch of leisurely wooing, or something that neither party remembers happening because it happened when they were both virtually asleep and one rolled into the other for comfort during a bad dream, I mean the years before that, when

one thing led to another and conclusions were somehow
reached before choices were made, when you became
a man in an altered condition as a result of a slip of
the tongue, or a moment of inattention. They felt more
like lapses than choices – one lapsed into the future as
possibly one lapses into infidelity, or into bankruptcy,
or into death –[12]

It is the almost accidental, even incidental nature of a lived
life that fascinates and saddens us. The way some of us
missed it while we were living it and now, getting near the
end like Simon Gray, wished we'd paid more attention at
the time, so that we could at least remember what it was
we were missing while we were missing it. Musing about
photography, Gray replays Larkin:

. . . the present never seems worth photographing, only
the past, when it's too late, which is why I suppose I've
so few photographs – Now of course I wish I'd taken
lots, especially of my parents, especially of my mother,
my mother in her prime, to block out the memory of
her skeletal hand clinging to mine, and I determined
not to look at my watch until I did, a swift, casual glance
down at my wrist. 'Oh', she said, in an anxious whisper,
'don't go yet, Si, stay a little while longer'. 'I can't', I
said, 'I have to pick Ben up from his nursery school'.
She held her hand out to retain me. I held it to my lips,
kissed her quickly on the forehead and left. I had enough
time, more than enough time to get to the nursery
school, so I walked along Putney towpath, and thought
about the kind of son I was, who would deprive his

dying mother of a few more minutes, that's all she'd
claimed, a few more minutes of his company. I still
don't know why I wouldn't stay. It wasn't coldness of
heart or fear of seeing her so extremely ill and dying.
There had just been an undeniable impulse to remove
myself. Inexplicable that it comes back to me now, as
it did one afternoon last summer on Spetses when,
drying after a swim, I watched a tiny old lady sitting in
the rim of the sea, picking stones out of the water,
looking at them, putting them back, not childishly but
like a child, and my eyes filled with tears of shame. I
am now nearly ten years older than she was when she
died, I've had all those years more than she had, and I
hadn't given her a few minutes of those years, on an
impulse . . .[13]

That is a shame I recognise from my own life. Looking
back, I am sorry I lived my life in such an eschatological,
purposeful rush, not having realised that it is the journey
not the journey's end that matters. Simon Gray regretted
denying his dying mother a few more minutes of his time.
What I most regret is not paying enough attention to my
children when they were young. By the time I looked up,
they were gone. If you live long enough you get forgiven
and get them all back, and that has happened to me. But
what you don't get back are the years of inattention, the
years you were looking away, the years you were looking
ahead instead of looking around.

If we are to love our lives and say yes to how we lived
them, how are we to incorporate the hurts we inflicted
and the mistakes we made? It means we must identify and

confess them. It means we are committed to lives of self-examination, reporting the facts of the case like a careful journalist of the soul. This is what the good poets do. And one of their favourite metaphors is the journey. We have encountered it already in Homer and Virgil. We encounter it again in the Egyptian poet Cavafy, using the same myth of Odysseus's long voyage home from Troy:

As you set out for Ithaka
hope your road is a long one,
full of adventure, full of discovery.
Laistrygonians, Cyclops,
angry Poseidon – don't be afraid of them:
you'll never find things like that on your way
as long as you keep your thoughts raised high,
as long as a rare excitement
stirs your spirit and your body.
Laistrygonians, Cyclops,
wild Poseidon – you won't encounter them
unless you bring them along inside your soul,
unless your soul sets them up in front of you.

Hope your road is a long one.
May there be many summer mornings when,
with what pleasure, what joy,
you enter harbours you're seeing for the first time;
may you stop at Phoenician trading stations
to buy fine things,
mother of pearl and coral, amber and ebony,
sensual perfume of every kind –
as many sensual perfumes as you can;

THE HEART OF THINGS

and may you visit many Egyptian cities
to learn and go on learning from their scholars.

Keep Ithaka always in your mind.
Arriving there is what you're destined for.
But don't hurry the journey at all.
Better if it lasts for years,
so you're old by the time you reach the island,
wealthy with all you've gained on the way,
not expecting Ithaka to make you rich.

Ithaka gave you the marvellous journey.
Without her you wouldn't have set out.
She has nothing left to give you now.

And if you find her poor, Ithaka won't have fooled
  you.
Wise as you will have become, so full of experience,
you'll have understood by then what these Ithakas
  mean.[14]

Cavafy was one of the poets who gave me a poem just
when I needed it, a poem not for the whole of life – such
as 'Ithaka' – but for an important moment, the way
Laurence Binyon gave me 'The Burning of the Leaves'
just when it was needed. It was Cavafy's 'The God
Abandons Antony' that found me when God was abandoning me or I was abandoning God: it gave me courage.

At midnight, when suddenly you hear
an invisible procession going by

with exquisite music, voices,
don't mourn your luck that's failing now,
work gone wrong, your plans
all proving deceptive – don't mourn them
    uselessly:
as one long prepared, and graced with courage,
say goodbye to her, the Alexandria that is leaving.
Above all, don't fool yourself, don't say
it was a dream, your ears deceived you:
don't degrade yourself with empty hopes like these.
As one long prepared, and full of courage,
as is right for you who were given this kind of city,
go firmly to the window
and listen with deep emotion,
but not with the whining, the pleas of a coward;
listen – your final pleasure – to the voices,
to the exquisite music of that strange procession,
and say goodbye to her, to the Alexandria you are
    losing.[15]

Sometimes it is not a whole poem. Not even a verse. It can be a single line that gives what is needed. I came across such a line when I was reading Iain Crichton Smith's *Selected Poems*. I wasn't particularly grabbed by the poem itself – 'She Teaches Lear' – but in the third line of the last verse it was waiting for me:

From our own weakness only are we kind.[16]

Of course! We can read our lives through the prism of heroism or defeat or resignation or shame. But only admitting our own weaknesses will make us kind, help us identify with others of our kind and act as kin to kin. And it has to apply to our relationship with the self, *our-self*. We have to learn how to be kin or kind to ourselves. It's a hard one to pull off. Thrown into existence, loaded with tendencies and dispositions we didn't ask for, we play the hand we are dealt, usually not very well. But we are not the only ones who failed. It has been true of every generation that passed over the face of the earth. All have fallen short. Yet there have always been some who looked with compassion on their fellow voyagers. They understood their travails, their shortcomings, and knew the unremembered memories they brought on board with them. We call them metaphysicians, soul-poets, artists who understand and love their own kind. One of them was called Jesus. His poem for us was called 'Forgiveness'. And like all necessary poetry, we find it when we need it. He used two different verbs for it. One was *aphiemi*, which means letting someone off a debt; the other was *apoluo*, meaning to liberate or let someone out of jail; or redeem, as in releasing someone from slavery.

It is interesting that he used tough words from the economic and political sphere, not soft phrases from escapist spirituality. For Jesus, forgiveness was a revolutionary act. But it was also a metaphor. It was a revolutionary act, because it recognised how the economic system was stacked against the poor, and always had been. An illuminating recent example from world politics was the decision to forgive what was known at the time as 'third world debt'. Given the nature of the global economy, there was no way these so-called 'developing countries' could earn their way out of their debt to the international market system, so if they were to be players in the market at all, part of the international political community, they had to be enabled to start afresh: their debts had to be forgiven. That was the kind of revolution Jesus was calling for, and it is just as appropriate in today's economy as it was then.

But forgiveness was also a metaphor for the need to release the debts and imprisonments we inflict on each other in our personal lives. We arrive on board loaded with urges and needs that cause us to fall into damaging transactions with each other. In his interpretation of Nietzsche's *amor fati,* Walter Kaufmann reminded us:

> That I am here, now, doing this – that depends on an awe-inspiring series of antecedent events, on millions of seemingly accidental moves and decisions, both by myself and many others whose moves and decisions in turn depended on yet other people. And our very existence, our being as we are, required that our parents had to choose each other, not anyone else, and beget us at the precise moment when we were actually begotten; and the same consideration applies to their parents, and to all our ancestors, going back indefinitely.

We are born with all that inherited past pressing through us. Our tiny life is the point or opening through which it flows into and – at our death – out of time into the realm of the forgotten. On one level, the accumulated past that flows through us does not care for or about us, probably does not even know us. We are its instruments, though over time we have become its conscious instruments. We know ourselves, know our-*self*. But only slowly, if at all, do we discover how we became who we are, with all that pressure from the past flowing into us and causing us to become the person we became. In the process of all that self-making we accumulate huge levels of moral and personal debt to those we have hurt, however unwittingly, in the complicated thrust of living out who we were becoming as we sped towards our own dying. And we either learn to forgive all that debt or carry it as grievance to the grave. If we choose to live in grievance – a valid choice – we lock ourselves away. If we forgive the debts, we open the gate and get back in the game.

Jesus thought the unforgiven and unforgiving life were not worth living. It was up to us, of course, but if we chose forgiveness it had to be habitual. Not seven times, but seventy times seven – always! It had to be a habitual way of being towards others and towards ourselves. It is a way of paradox, of course. We have to forgive those who cannot forgive us – and understand why. The forgiven and forgiving person has a certain lightness of being, in spite of the crushing weight of all that history pushing into and through us. Transcendence is the word. Getting above it or over it, including getting over ourselves. A refusal to let heaviness and grievance and hate be the only or the dominant game. All that locking up, that banging away, that resentment, those fists in your face! Lighten up, forgiveness smiles. Yes, forgiveness *smiles*. Forgiveness is a lightsome thing. Come on, it cries, lighten up. The other great thing about forgiveness is that it gives NOW back to us, the present moment, the only moment we are ever *in*. It puts an end to eschatological thinking, revenge thinking, the kind of thinking that robs us of the joy of the present moment because it is always looking back in anger or forward to revenge. Remember Isaiah Berlin . . .

> If you look . . . for some other goal, the moment will come when the singer stops and then you will only have memories and vain regrets because, instead of listening, you were waiting for something else . . .

> *Instead of listening, you were waiting for something else . . .*

That sounds like me as I draw nearer to port: memories and regrets. And not just because I wasn't listening or because I was waiting for something else. I was:

> not so much waiting
>   as *searching*.
> For the hidden,
> the maybe not there,
> the romantic's prayer.

> On the hills as a boy,
>   alone,
> looking for what was
> at the heart of things,

finding only traces,
like the impress
a hare leaves
on the heather,

or like the universe itself,
arriving from nowhere
    for no reason,
coming up with us,
hunters for meaning
and the purpose of things,

chasing the hare,
we never catch up with,
wondering if it exists
or whether, somehow,
it had already been killed,

as Nietzsche claimed,

that what was holiest and mightiest
of all that the world had yet owned
had bled to death under our knives,

now there could be no comfort
    for the world's sorrow,
no final resolution of its pain,
at the end of the story
no one was writing.

FORGIVING

It isn't atheism, this sad anger,
the atheism of those
glad there's no meaning,
and proud to be in on
the empty secret.

Let them be, the
Gospelling Atheists,
they have their reward;
    but me,
saddened by God's absence,
what's mine?

It should be *gratitude*.
Wherever the world came from,
I got here too, didn't I?
    Lived my days,
loved and was loved,

I, who would have
drowned in Africa,
had the relenting ocean
not thrown me back
on shore,

I, who walked the hills,
I, who saw white hares dancing
in the snow on Lammermuir,
should be grateful for life,
    even as it passes.

Leaving the Usher Hall,
I say, wasn't that glorious,
not, I'm sad that's over.
Nevertheless,
      over it soon will be,

like the lights going up
at the Children's Matinee,
and the words on the screen
I never wanted to see:
      THE END,
sending me out
onto the wet streets . . .

      endings,
there were always endings,
but I was always glad I went.

Now as my own life
spools its last reel,
I'm still not sure
if Someone was behind it,
like the projectionist
in the old picture houses
I went to and loved
as a boy.

Maybe at The End,
      somehow,
I'll know.

But wasn't it great,
the show, I tell myself,
as the lights come up
and the curtains
start to close?

It was, it WAS!

AMEN.

ENDNOTES

Preface
1. Holloway, Richard. *Leaving Alexandria*. Edinburgh: Canongate, 2013.
2. Montaigne, Michel de. Quoted in *The Oxford Dictionary of Quotations*. Oxford: Oxford University Press, 2014, p. 355.

Chapter 1
1. Boland, Eavan. 'The Necessity for Irony'. In: *The Lost Land*. London: W.W. Norton, 1998.
2. Freud, Sigmund. *On Murder, Mourning and Melancholia*. London: Penguin Classics, 2005, p. 203.
3. Virgil, *The Aeneid*. Book 1, 1.462.
4. Freud, *On Murder, Meaning and Melancholia*, p. 203.
5. Milton, John. 'L'Allegro'. In: *The Oxford Book of English Verse*. Oxford: Oxford University Press, 1939, p. 329.
6. Milton, John. 'Il Penseroso'. In: *The Oxford Book of English Verse*, p. 334.
7. Boland, Eavan. 'The Lost Art of Letter Writing'. *New Yorker*, 25 August 2014.
8. Morris, Jan. *Trieste and the Meaning of Nowhere*. London: Faber and Faber, 2002, p. 3.

9. Graham, W. S. 'Loch Thom'. In: Matthew Francis (ed.), *New Collected Poems*. London: Faber and Faber, 2004.

10. Freud, *On Murder, Mourning and Melancholia,* p. 203.

11. Orwell, George. *The Collected Essays, Journalism and Letters of George Orwell*. Volume 1. London: Penguin Books, 1970, p. 29.

12. Orwell, *The Collected Essays*, pp. 23–4.

13. Orwell, *The Collected Essays*, p. 25

14. Newsome, David. *On the Edge of Paradise: A.C. Benson Diarist*. London: John Murray, 1980, p. 1.

15. Orwell, *The Collected Essays*, p. 26.

16. Orwell, *The Collected Essays*, p. 26.

17. Orwell, *The Collected Essays*, p. 25.

18. Niebuhr, Reinhold. *Leaves from the Notebook of a Tamed Cynic*. Westminster: John Knox Press, 1990.

19. This poem, and unattributed poems that close following chapters, are written by Richard Holloway and published here for the first time.

Chapter 2

1. St Vincent Millay, Edna. 'Dirge Without Music'. In: *Collected Poems*. London: HarperCollins, 1958. © 1928, 1955 by Edna St Vincent Millay and Norma Millay Ellis. Reprinted with permission of Elizabeth Barnett and Holly Peppe, Literary Executors, the Millay Society.

2. Betjeman, John. 'Old Friends'. In: *High and Low*. London: John Murray, 1966, p. 11.

3. Wilson, A.N. *Betjeman*. London: Hutchinson, 2006, p. 314.

4. *The Scottish Book of Common Prayer*. Cambridge: Cambridge University Press, 1929, p. 459.

5. Scott Holland, Henry. From the sermon 'Death the King of Terrors', delivered in St Paul's Cathedral, Whitsunday 1910, at: <https://www.familyfriendpoems. com/poem/death-is-nothing-at-all-by-henry-scott-holland>

6. Larkin, Philip. 'Dockery and Son'. In *Collected Poems*. London: The Marvell Press, and Faber and Faber, 2003, p. 109.

7. Woolf, Virginia. *The Waves*. London: Penguin Classics, 2000, p. 20.

8. Woolf, *The Waves*, p. 114.

9. Lee, Hermione. *Virginia Woolf*. London: Vintage, 1997, p. 759.

10. Woolf, *The Waves*, p. 228.

11. Fitzgerald, F. Scott. *The Great Gatsby*. London: Penguin Modern Classics, 2000, p. 166.

12. Larkin, Philip. 'Lines on a Young Lady's Photograph Album'. In *Collected Poems*, p. 43.

13. Fitzgerald, *The Great Gatsby*, p. 166.

14. Clampitt, Amy. 'Witness'. In: *What the Light Was Like*. New York: Knopf Poetry Series, 1983.

15. Auden, W.H. 'In Memory of W.B. Yeats'. In: *W.H. Auden Collected Poems*. London: Faber and Faber, 1976, p. 197.

Chapter 3

1. Binyon, Laurence. 'Fetching the Wounded'. In: Paul O'Prey (ed.), *Poems of Two Wars: Laurence Binyon*. London: Dare-Gale Press, 2016, p. 35.

2. O'Prey, *Poems of Two Wars: Laurence Binyon*, p. 15.

3. Binyon, Laurence. 'The Burning of the Leaves'. In:

Larkin, Philip (ed.), *The Oxford Book of Twentieth Century English Verse*. Oxford: Oxford University Press, 1973, p. 102.

4. Owen, Wilfred. 'Preface'. In: Day Lewis, Cecil (ed.), *The Collected Poems of Wilfred Owen*. London: Chatto and Windus, 1963, p. 31.

5. Auden, W.H. 'September 1, 1939'. In: *Another Time*. London: Random House, 1940.

6. Owen, Wilfred. 'Fragment: I Saw His Round Mouth's Crimson'. In: *The Collected Poems of Wilfred Owen*, p. 110.

7. Weil, Simone. *An Anthology*. Edited and introduced by Siân Miles. New York: Grove Press, 1986, p. 163.

8. Housman, A.E. In: F. C. Harwood (ed.) *Poetry and Prose: A Selection*. London: Hutchinson Educational, 1971, p. 173.

9. Gibbon, Lewis. Grassic *Sunset Song*. Edinburgh: Canongate, 2006, p. 255.

10. Gibbon, *Sunset Sing,* p. 154.

11. Gibbon, *Sunset Song,* p. 167.

12. Gibbon, *Sunset Song,* p. 167.

13. Gibbon, Lewis. Grassic *Cloud Howe,* London: Hutchinson, 1946, p. 207.

14. Owen, Wilfred. 'The Parable of the Old Man and the Young'. In: *The Collected Poems of Wilfred Owen*, p. 42

15. Wilson, A.N. *After the Victorians: 1901–1953*. London: Hutchinson, 2005, p. 127.

16. Bilgere, George. 'At the Vietnam Memorial'. In: *The Poetry Anthology 1912–2002*. London: Copper Beech Press, 2002.

17. Harrison, Robert Pogue. *The Dominion of the Dead*. Chicago: University of Chicago Press, 2003, p. 136.

18. Harrison, *The Dominion of the Dead*, p. 137.
19. Steiner, George. *Errata*. London: Phoenix, 1997, p. 13.
20. Borges, Jorge Luis. 'Possession of Yesterday'. In: David Curzon (ed.), *Modern Poems on the Bible*. Philadelphia: The Jewish Publication Society, 1994, p. 89.
21. All the information here comes from O'Prey, Paul (ed.), *Poems of Two Wars: Laurence Binyon*.
22. Binyon, Laurence. 'Poem IV'. In: O' Prey (ed.), *Poems of Two Wars: Laurence Binyon*, p. 92.
23. Binyon, Laurence. 'Poem II'. In: O' Prey (ed), *Poems of Two Wars: Laurence Binyon*, p. 89.

Chapter 4

1. Shelley, Percy Bysshe. 'Ozymandias'. In: *The New Oxford Book of English Verse 1250–1950*. Oxford: Clarendon Press, 1972, p. 580.
2. Matthew, 23:37–38.
3. Lamentations, 1:1–2.
4. Amichai, Yehuda. 'Ecology of Jerusalem'. In: Bloch, Chana and Stephen Mitchell (trans.), *The Selected Poetry of Yehuda Amichai*. Berkeley: University of California Press, 1996, p. 136.
5. Lamentations, 1:12.
6. Hollis, Edward. *The Secret Life of Buildings*. London: Portobello Books, 2009, p. 3.
7. Morgan, Edwin. 'Glasgow Sonnet'. In: *Collected Poems*. Manchester: Carcanet Press, 1990, p. 168.
8. Morgan, Edwin. 'Old Gorbals'. In: *A Book of Lives*. Manchester: Carcanet Press, 2007, p. 47.
9. Morgan, Edwin. 'Glasgow Green'. In: *Collected Poems*, p. 168.

Chapter 5

1. Nietzsche, Friedrich. *Ecce Homo*, II.10, Translated by R.J. Hollingdale. London: Penguin Books, 1979, p. 68.

2. Prideaux, Sue. *I Am Dynamite! A Life of Friedrich Nietzsche*. London: Faber and Faber, 2018, p. 220.

3. Borges, Jorge Luis. 'Possession of Yesterday'. In: David Curzon (ed.), *Modern Poems on the Bible*, Philadelphia: The Jewish Publication Society, 1994, p. 89.

4. Housman, A.E. 'With Rue My Heart is Laden'. In: F.C. Harwood (ed.), *Poetry and Prose: A Selection*. London: Hutchinson Educational, 1971, p. 102.

5. Housman, *Poetry and Prose: A Selection*, p. 32.

6. Housman, *Poetry and Prose: A Selection*, p. 34.

7. Housman, A.E. 'The Farms of Home Lie Lost in Even'. In: *Poetry and Prose: A Selection*, p. 163.

8. Housman, A.E. 'Loveliest of Trees, the Cherry Now'. In: *Poetry and Prose: A Selection*, p. 47.

9. Wilson, A.N. *Betjeman*. London: Hutchinson, 2006, p. 101.

10. Betjeman, John. 'Death of King George V'. In: *Collected Poems*. London: John Murray, 2006, p. 35.

11. MacNeice, Louis. 'Carrickfergus'. In: *Selected Poems*. London: Faber and Faber, 1964, p. 69.

12. MacNeice, Louis. 'Autobiography'. In: *Selected Poems*, p. 183.

13. MacNeice, Louis. 'Snow'. In: *Selected Poems*, p. 30.

14. From a story described to the author by Gail McConnell, lecturer in the School of English at Queen's University, Belfast.

15. Mahon, Derek. 'In Carrowdore Churchyard'. In: *New Collected Poems*. Ireland: The Gallery Press, 2011, p. 19.

16. Mahon, Derek. 'Brian Moore's Belfast'. In: *New Collected Poems*, p. 292.
17. Mahon, Derek. 'Yaddo, or A Month in the Country'. In: *New Collected Poems*, p. 157.
18. MacNeice, Louis. 'Prayer Before Birth'. In: *Selected Poems*, p.74.

Chapter 6

1. Lawrence, D.H. 'Self-Pity'. In: Larkin, Philip (ed.), *The Oxford Book of Twentieth Century English Verse*. Oxford: Oxford University Press, 1973, p. 193.
2. Doty, Mark. 'Migratory'. In: *Being Alive*. Northumberland: Bloodaxe Books, 2004, p. 44.
3. Greville, Fulke (Lord Brooke). 'Chorus Sacerdotum'. In: *The New Oxford Book of English Verse 1250–1950*, Oxford: Clarendon Press, 1972, p. 118.
4. Quoted in Hermione Lee, *Tom Stoppard: A Life*. London: Faber and Faber, 2020, p. 78.
5. Genesis, 3:9–12.
6. Nietzsche, Friedrich. *The Birth of Tragedy*. London: Penguin Classics, 1993, p.53.
7. Quoted in Lee. *Tom Stoppard: A Life*, p. 289.
8. Koethe, John. 'Expulsion from the Garden'. In: *North Point North: New and Selected Poems*. New York: Perennial, 2003, p. 6.
9. Nietzsche, Friedrich. *Ecce Homo*, II.10. Translated by R.J. Hollingdale. London: Penguin Books, 1979, p. 68.
10. Kaufmann, Walter. *Nietzsche: Philosopher, Psychologist, Antichrist*. New Jersey: Princeton University Press, 1974, p. 282.
11. Eliot, T.S. 'Burnt Norton'. In: *The Complete Poems and*

Plays. New York: Harcourt, Brace and Company, 1952, p. 117.

12. Gray, Simon. *The Last Cigarette*. London: Granta, 2008, p. 196.

13. Gray, *The Last Cigarette*, p. 149.

14. Cavafy, C.P. 'Ithaka'. In: *C.P Cavafy: Collected Poems*. Edmund Keeley and Philip Sherrard (trans.). London: Chatto and Windus, 1998, p. 29.

15. Cavafy, C.P. 'The God Abandons Antony'. In *C.P Cavafy: Collected Poems*, p. 27.

16. Crichton Smith, Iain. 'She Teaches Lear'. In: *Selected Poems*. Manchester: Carcanet, 1985, p. 54.

ACKNOWLEDGEMENTS

I have dedicated this book to my friend and colleague, Alastair Hulbert, because he played an important part in its gradual formation over the years. Alastair was Warden of Scottish Churches House in Dunblane from 2003 to 2008, and during his time there he and I organised a number of study weekends focused on reading, studying and sometimes writing poetry. Guided by Robyn Marsack, who was then Director of the Scottish Poetry Library in Crichton's Close, off the Canongate in Edinburgh, we ranged widely in our study, and a number of the poems that appear in this book were first introduced to me during those weekends. I owe a duty of thanks to both Alastair and Robyn.

I'd also like to register my thanks to my editor at Canongate, Simon Thorogood, for all his care and attention in getting this book out; as well as to my agents Caroline Dawnay and Sophie Scard at United Agents, for their affectionate stewardship over the years.

Getting an anthology like this through the process of achieving and paying for permission to publish the material quoted is both tedious and complicated, so I owe an enormous Thank You to Leila Cruickshank, Managing Editor at Canongate, and to Helen Bartlett, freelance permissions editor, for getting it done so competently and expeditiously.

PERMISSION CREDITS

and Faber Ltd (2016). Reproduced by permission by David Higham Associates.

'Autobiography' from *Collected Poems* by Louis MacNeice, published by Faber and Faber Ltd (2016). Reproduced by permission by David Higham Associates.

'Snow' from *Collected Poems* by Louis MacNeice, published by Faber and Faber Ltd (2016). Reproduced by permission by David Higham Associates.

'Prayer Before Birth' from *Collected Poems* by Louis MacNeice, published by Faber and Faber Ltd (2016). Reproduced by permission by David Higham Associates.

'Carrowdore' from *The Poems* by Derek Mahon, published by The Gallery Press (2021). By kind permission of the author's Estate c/o The Gallery Press, Loughcrew, Oldcastle, County Meath, Ireland.

'Brian Moores' Belfast' from in *The Poems* by Derek Mahon, published by The Gallery Press (2021). By kind permission of the author's Estate c/o The Gallery Press, Loughcrew, Oldcastle, County Meath, Ireland.

'Yaddo, or A Month in the Country' from in *The Poems* by Derek Mahon, published by The Gallery Press (2021). By kind permission of the author's Estate c/o The Gallery Press, Loughcrew, Oldcastle, County Meath, Ireland.

'Dirge Without Music' from *Collected Poems* by Edna St. Vincent Millay. Copyright 1928, © 1955 by Edna St. Vincent Millay and Norma Millay Ellis. Reprinted with the permission of The Permissions Company, LLC on behalf of Holly Peppe, Literary Executor, The Edna St. Vincent Millay Society. www.millay.org.

Excerpts from 'Glasgow Green' from *Collected Poems* by Edwin Morgan, published by Carcanet Press (1990). Copyright © 1990 Edwin Morgan. Reproduced by permission of Carcanet Press, Manchester, UK.

Excerpt from 'Old Gorbals' from *A Book of Lives* by Edwin Morgan, published by Carcanet Press (2007). Copyright © 2007 Edwin Morgan. Reproduced by permission of Carcanet Press, Manchester, UK.

Letter to Leonard Woolf from Virginia Woolf, March 28, 1941 from *Collected Letters (v.6) (Leave the Letters Till We're Dead)* published by Chatto & Windus (1994). Copyright © 1975, 1976, 1977, 1978, 1979, 1980, 1989 by Quentin Bell and Angelica Garnett. Reproduced by permission of The Society of Authors as the Literary Representative of the Estate of Virginia Woolf; The Random House Group Ltd; and Houghton Mifflin Harcourt Publishing Company. All rights reserved.

IMAGE CREDITS